Revelation
Book of Mystery and Majesty

by

Dr. Kelly Carr

Franklin Publishing

Greenville, Texas

Revelation

Book of Mystery and Majesty

Original Copyright © 1998

Dr. Kelly Carr

Except where otherwise indicated, all Scripture quotations in this book are from the New American Standard Bible, 1960, 1962, 1963, 1968, 1971, 1972, 1973, 1975, and 1977 by the Lockman Foundation, and are used by permission.

Franklin Publishing

Greenville, Texas

Printed in the United States of America Copyright © 2014 Kelly Carr

2nd Printing 2014

ISBN: 0692232427
ISBN-13: 978-0692232422

TESTIMONIALS

"Too often pastors shun preaching on prophecy in general and the Book of Revelation in particular. Here is a thorough and practical guide to Revelation that will render them without excuse. Prepared by a pastor for pastors (and other Bible teachers) the author has produced a sane and scholarly study that is both expository and applicational. It interprets Revelation from a futurist (premillennial) viewpoint. I am pleased to recommend this helpful volume on a difficult but understandable book of the Bible by my former student, Kelly Carr."

Dr. Don Campbell,
President, 1986-1994
Dallas Theological Seminary

"It was a great joy to receive a brand new study book on Revelation by Dr. Kelly Carr. ... It is the best I've ever seen for Pastors and Sunday School Teachers. I would recommend it to every Pastor and every church in our great convention.

Dr. Carr is a Bible, scholar yet can communicate the great truths in this study. ... If I were a Pastor, I would hurriedly order this study from him for a Wednesday night prayer meeting or Sunday night study. You will find it to be premillennial, pretribulational, and evangelistic. If I can offer any other help to you please call me."

Walter K. Ayers
Southern Baptist Evangelist
972-475-2600

"Revelation has been developed by Dr. Carr in a most interesting and insightful way. In a well-ordered and carefully researched curriculum, he has honored its majesty without removing the mystery that has attracted the church throughout history. The lessons are eye-catching and easy-to-read with frequent applications to take the student from text to life. I highly recommend the work for all lay students of the Word."

Dr. Lanier Burns
Chairman, Theology Department
Dallas Theological Seminary

"Congratulations, you have a good commentary. There are many commentaries dealing with The Revelation, but this is one of the clearest and most understandable I have ever perused. I believe it will be especially helpful to young ministers just entering the preaching force.

It is biblically and carefully based and presents 'truth' in a manner that it clear. I believe also that it is simple enough for the young Christian just wanting to come to an understanding on this very exciting book of the Bible.

Your presentation is smooth and compelling. It should get a wide hearing from the brethren in our churches. It made me wish that I had had it in my hands many years ago when I first started trying to preach through Revelation. ..."

Dr. Harold O'Chester
Pastor, Great Hills Baptist Church
Austin, Texas

"Dr. Kelly Carr has produced a fine series of expository outlines that will enable a student or teacher to see the synthesis and be guided toward the analysis of this great book of God's revelation. The treatment is balanced and will provide a helpful guide for those interested in knowing God's plan for the future."

Dr. Mark L. Bailey
Vice President for Academic Affairs
Dallas Theological Seminary

"Enjoyed your study in Revelation. It should be popular and simple for churches to use."

Harold W. Poage
Vice President for Institutional Advancement
Midwestern Baptist Theological Seminary

DEDICATION

This work is lovingly dedicated to my wife, Cindy, for all those early mornings when she was left alone so I could write, to Timothy, Andrew, and Rebecca Belle, who will never know how much Daddy misses them when he is gone, to the members of Dixon Baptist Church, the best church family in the world who allow me to practice my gifts, to the Auditorium Class which allowed me to teach these notes in the first place, and most of all to our Lord Jesus Christ whom Revelation is meant to reveal.

May this offering help to accomplish His intended desire.

ACKNOWLEDGMENTS

Grateful acknowledgment is made to the publishers for permission to quote from the following copyrighted material:

The Revelation of John: Volume 1 by William Barclay. Copyright 1976 by The Westminster Press.

The Rise of Babylon: Sign of the End Times by Charles H. Dyer with Angela Elwell Hunt copyright 1991 by Charles Dyer. Used by permission of Tyndale House Publishers, Inc. All rights reserved.

Revelation: Illustrated and Made Plain by Tim LaHaye. Copyright 1973, 1975 by Tim LaHaye. Used by permission of Zondervan Publishing House.

One World Under Anti-Christ by Peter Lalonde. Copyright 1991. Used by permission of Harvest House Publishers.

Racing Toward the Mark of the Beast by Peter and Paul Lalonde. Copyright 1994. Used by permission of Harvest House Publishers.

Reveling Through Revelation by J. Vernon McGee. Copyright 1962. Used by permission of Thru the Bible Radio.

Exploring Revelation by John Phillips. Copyright 1974, 1987 by John Phillips. Used by permission of publisher Loizeaux, Neptune, New Jersey.

Basic Theology by Charles C. Ryrie. Copyright 1986. Used by permission of Chariot Victor Publishing.

Revelation by Charles C. Ryrie. Copyright 1968. Used by permission of Moody Press.

A Revelation of Jesus Christ by J. B. Smith. Copyright 1961. Used by permission of Mennonite Publishing House.

The Book of Revelation by Lehman Strauss. Copyright 1964. Used by permission of Loizeaux Brothers, Inc. Neptune, New Jersey.

Letters to the Churches...Then and Now by Charles R. Swindoll. Copyright 1981. Used by permission of Insight for Living.

The Revelation of Jesus Christ by John F. Walvoord. Copyright 1966. Used by permission of Moody Press.

The King is Coming by H. L. Willmington. Copyright 1973, 1981, 1991 by Tyndale House Publishers, Inc. All rights reserved. Used by permission.

Illustration Digest Number 1, 1996 by A A Publishing. Copyright 1996. Used by permission.

TABLE OF CONTENTS

FOREWORD

Kelly Carr has written a fascinating study guide for Revelation that came out of a series of expository messages he preached at Dixon Baptist Church. He then adapted it into a six month study for his auditorium class. I believe when a book comes from the heart of a pastor, and is channeled to the public through the preaching of the pulpit, that book has a much greater chance of touching the hearts of its readers. This study guide of the book of Revelation has that opportunity to open up great insight and illumination to the readers. Beyond that, it can touch the readers' hearts and spirits and motivate them to faithfulness and to watching for His coming.

I am thrilled when graduates from Liberty go out and make their mark for God. Kelly Carr has been used greatly in preaching and teaching the Word of God. I remember him at Liberty University in our pioneer days, when our students did not have dormitories, but rather lived on Treasure Island in winterized cabins, and later in a downtown hotel that had been refurbished into a college dormitory. Kelly was a resident advisor for two years. It was while he was learning at Liberty and serving at Liberty, that his philosophy of ministry was shaped and directed.

I pray that God will bless this book with His anointing so that many people may fall in love with Jesus Christ, and study carefully His second coming. May God bless this book to its intended use, and may its ministry extend far beyond the State of Texas where Kelly pastors at Dixon Baptist Church.

Dr. Jerry Falwell, Founder/Chancellor

Liberty University, Lynchburg, Virginia (1998)

PREFACE

The Pastor, Sunday School teacher, or Bible study leader who desires to teach on the book of Revelation, can find many commentaries, but few real aids in teaching the book. This book is not meant to be a commentary on Revelation, though you will find it helpful in determining the meaning of the book. It is intended to be a study guide or a curriculum which will enable the Bible teacher to have an organized way to study and teach this valuable book.

This study is organized into 26 lessons. This makes it easy to teach the book in six months of weekly classes. Each lesson is organized in outline form so that it will be easy for a group of students to follow a teacher who is teaching from this format. The Student Guide, which may be purchased separately, is reproducible and has blanks for the student to fill in as the teacher leads the discussion. It also has the same page numbers as the Teacher's Guide so that both teacher and student will be on the same page. The reproducible format also allows the teacher to teach this series many times. The outline form also makes it helpful for the busy Pastor who desires to preach a sermon series on the book of Revelation. These outlines can be easily modified to fit your own preaching style.

Revelation was not intended to be unapproachable portion of Scripture. It is a wealth of information and inspiration for the believer, and a real motivation for the believer and unbeliever alike. The word, "revelation," actually means "to reveal." The book of Revelation is intended to reveal something about our Lord Jesus Christ and His plan for the future. Some parts of this book are admittedly very difficult to understand, but the great majority is very clear and easy to understand for the person who takes the Scripture literally. In fact, the thing that so many people find fearful about this book is that it is so clear about so many things. What many people do not realize about this great book is that it touches on so many great doctrines of the Bible, such as sin, salvation, the person of Christ, the church, and practical Christian living, as well as future things. Another thing that so many do not realize is the great contribution that Revelation makes in the area of worship. We see so many wonderful scenes of majestic worship in these chapters, and get a preview of some of the music of Heaven. The person who earnestly desires to understand worship cannot afford to neglect the study of Revelation. One must also keep in mind that Revelation was not merely written to satisfy the curiosity of complacent Christians. Rather, it was written to give hope and encouragement to Christians who were risking it all for Christ, and to motivate others to do the same.

Revelation is truly a "Book of Mystery and Majesty." It is my hope that whether you are a Pastor preparing to preach through Revelation, a Bible teacher preparing to teach through Revelation, or simply a Bible student desiring to come a an understanding of this great portion of God's word, this study will have our Lord's intended affect on you and all those with whom you share it.

Till He Comes!

Dr. Kelly F. Carr

INTRODUCTORY REMARKS

Some Striking Features of the Book of Revelation:

1. It is the only prophetic book in the New Testament (in contrast to 17 prophetic books in the Old Testament).

2. John, the writer, reaches farther back into eternity past than any other writer in Scripture (John 1:1-3). He reaches farther on into eternity future in the book of Revelation.

3. Special blessing is promised the readers of this book (Revelation 1:3). Likewise, a warning is issued to those who tamper with its contents (Revelation 22:18,19).

4. Revelation is not a sealed book (Revelation 22:10). Contrast Daniel 12:9. It is a revelation (apocalypse), which means unveiling.

5. It is a series of visions, expressed in symbols.

6. Revelation assumes a knowledge of the other 65 books of the Bible. Especially Genesis, Daniel, Zechariah, and Matthew.

7. This book is like a great union station where the great trunk lines of prophecy come in from other portions of Scripture. Revelation does not originate, but consummates.
    (from Reveling thru Revelation by J. Vernon McGee)

Contrasts between Genesis and Revelation:

Genesis-The commencement of Heaven and Earth (1:1)
Revelation- The consummation of Heaven and Earth (21:1)

Genesis- The entrance of sin and the curse (3:1-19)
Revelation- The end of sin and the curse (21:27, 22:3)

Genesis- The dawn of Satan and his activities (3:1-7)
Revelation- The doom of Satan and his activities (20:10)

Genesis- The tree of life is relinquished (2:9, 3:24)
Revelation- The tree of life is regained (22:2)

Genesis- Death makes its entrance (2:17, 5:5)
Revelation- Death makes its exit (21:4)

Genesis- Sorrow begins (3:16)
Revelation- Sorrow is banished (21:4)   (from Revelation by Lehman Straus)

Common Attitudes Toward Revelation:

1. It cannot be understood. Therefore, it should not be taught or preached. It has divided Christians.

2. It is the only book worth studying. Therefore some scan every detail of the book, set dates, and concoct fanciful interpretations.   (from Revelation by Charles Ryrie)

3. It is irrelevant to everyday life. It has no here and now application. This could not be more erroneous. The heavenly visions of Revelation have great earthly value. Their purpose is not to confuse, fascinate, or entertain us but to motivate us to live Christianly in an alien hostile world.   (from Letters to the Churches, Chuck Swindoll)

4. The proper attitude is that it is important and profitable like all Scripture (2 Timothy 3:16). But it is not the only book in the Bible. It is given by God in such a way as to be understandable by Christians.

Four Major Viewpoints for Interpreting Revelation:

1. The Preterist view maintains that the prophecies of the book took place during the time of the Roman Empire and in the lifetime of John.

2. The Historical view understands the book as portraying a panorama of the history of the Church from the days of John to the end time.

3. The Idealist view spiritualizes the book according to the allegorical method and considers the book a pictorial unfolding of the eternal struggle of the forces of good and evil between Christianity and paganism. (Disneyland approach)

*4. The Futurist view maintains that the majority of the book is future yet to be fulfilled, revealing the realization of the eternal program of God in the coming ages. This method best accords with the literal method of hermeneutics which will be followed here. "the things which shall take place after these things." (from class notes Dallas Theological Seminary Professor Mark Bailey)

   "A recent statement is, 'If the literal sense makes good sense, seek no other sense.' And it may be added, every other sense is usually nonsense. It is generally the case that if words do not mean what they say, no one can say what they mean." (from Revelation by J. B. Smith)

LESSON 1
PRELUDE TO THE END
(REVELATION 1:1-3)

Introduction:

1. We are living at the end of the old age and the threshold of the age to come.

2. Revelation answers the question "What on earth is God doing for heaven's sake."

3. This book pictures Christ taking the throne and defeating Satan, His rival to the throne.

4. It is a source of encouragement for believers to remain faithful in times of persecution. There is coming a day of vindication.

5. It is a severe warning for unbelievers.

6. It was occasioned by the horrible crisis of the end of the first century. The national persecution of Christians under the Roman Emperor, Domitian, who exiled John to Patmos.
   Ch 5-

I. The Presentation of the Book 1:1-2

   A. The "Revelation"

   Greek word = "apocalupsis" It does not mean "the end" or "tragedy." It means literally "the unveiling" or "the revealing."

   B. The Relay

   1. God the Father   "God"   (cf. Matt. 24:36)

   2. God the Son "Him"

   "Signified" means he used signs and symbols.

   3. By His Angel   "His angel"

   Why the Angel? The angel was necessary to explain the message to John.

   4. His Bond-servant John   "John"

   This refers to the author, the apostle John.

1

    5. His Bond-servants "His bondservants"

This refers not only to the believers living in John's day, but also to all the saints of the ages, including the present generation.

II. The Purpose of the Book 1:1

"to show to His bond-servants the things which must shortly take place."

    A. The Future Sense of the Revelation

The tense of the verb ("take place") is definitely future.

    B. The Certainty of the Revelation

"Must" here indicates the certainty of that which is discussed.

    C. The Speed of the Revelation

"Shortly" comes from the Greek word "tachei." It means "quickly,"

"speedily," or "suddenly." Our English word "tachometer" is a device to measure velocity.

III. The Promise of the Book 1:3

    A. A Blessing

There is a three-fold blessing of the book. It is a Beatitude. There are 7 Beatitudes in Revelation (1:3/ 14:13/ 16:15/ 19:19/ 20:6/ 22:7,14). (cf. Appendix 3)

        1. "He who reads"

This is singular. Not everyone had a Bible in John's day.

        2. "Those who hear the words of this prophecy"

This is plural. "Prophecy" is an indication that this book deals with the future.

        3. "Those who heed the things which are written in it"

"Heed" means to accept something as true, and to live accordingly.

    B. A Warning   "for the time is near"

"the time"="kairos" This means a period of time.

"near"= "at hand" It means prophetically near not chronologically near (cf. Rom. 13:10/ Rev. 22:10). His coming is "imminent."

IV. The Plan of the Book   1:19

John is commanded to "write". In this verse we are given the divine outline of the book of Revelation. (cf. Appendix 2)

    A. "the things which you have seen"

This refers to the vision of Christ John sees in chapter 1.

    B. "the things which are"

This refers to the seven churches that existed in John's time and are addressed in chapters 2 and 3.

C. "the things which shall take place after these things"

This refers to everything that takes place after chapter 4 which begins with the phrase, "after these things."

Conclusion:

The opening verses of Revelation are a rich mine of blessing and promise to every believer. We see the importance of this message which God has gone to so much trouble to send to us. We are promised a tremendous blessing for reading and studying the book, and we are given the wonderful assurance that Jesus will return for His saints. His coming could be at any time. There is no prophecy that must be fulfilled, or sign that must precede His coming. His coming is imminent.

Are You Ready To Meet Him If He Comes Today?

Matt 5-16
2 Cor 4-6
54 thr of Seven
7 church 7. Letter

LESSON 2
A VISION OF CHRIST
(REVELATION 1:4-20)

THE SOURCE OF THE VISION 1:4-8

I. The Human Source 1:4

    A. The Scribe of the Revelation

The Apostle John is the human author. Every word of God has both a heavenly and a divine source (cf. 2 Peter 1:21).

    B. The Destination of the Revelation

The seven churches that are in Asia, modern day Turkey (cf. 1:11). There were more than 7 churches in Asia, but these 7 are singled out. The number 7 is used often in this book (e.g.. 7 churches, 7 angels, 7 stars, 7 bowls, 7 trumpets, etc.).

II. A Hopeful Salutation 1:4

"grace and peace from Him"

    A. "Grace" = The Greek word of greeting

    B. "Peace" = The Hebrew word of greeting

To the world this book deals with judgment and war, but to the believer it is a message of grace and peace.

III. The Heavenly Source 1:4b-8

This book claims a Trinitarian authorship.

    A. God the Father "from Him who is, and who was, and who is to come."

    B. God the Spirit   "the seven Spirits who are before His throne"

The "seven Spirits" is probably a reference to the fullness of the Holy Spirit since seven is often used to signify fullness (cf. Isa. 11:2).

    C. God the Son   "and from Jesus Christ"

Jesus= His earthly name. It means "savior."

Christ= His Messianic title. It means "the Anointed One."

   1. The Position of the Son 1:5b

      a. Faithful Witness - looks to the past - speaks of His office as Prophet

      b. Firstborn of the Dead - looks to the present - speaks of His office as Priest

      literally "from the dead"   Others were raised in corruption. Jesus was raised in incorruption.

      "firstborn"= "prototokos" Not just first in order, but He is first in priority.

      c. Ruler of the Kings of the Earth - looks to the future - speaks of His office as King

      He is sovereign even now, but a day is coming when He will return to reign as King of Kings and Lord of Lords (Rev. 19:16).

   2. The Performance of the Son 1:5c-7

      a. His Performance in the Past 1:5c

      He loved us = Present tense

      He released us from our sins = Past tense

      b. His Performance in the Present 1:6

      He has made us to be a kingdom of priests

      He has given us a Princely Majesty, and Priestly Ministry

      "dominion"= "the right to rule"

      "Amen" Greek transliteration of the Hebrew word. It means "so be it," or "be it true." (If it as OK for John to get excited and say "Amen," I guess it's OK for us.)

      c. His Performance in the Future 1:7

      "He is coming" = Certainty

      How? "With the clouds" refers to the Second Coming (cf. Acts 1:9-11). (Not the Rapture.)

      "every eye will see Him" (Not a secret coming.) The whole world will know.

      "those who pierced Him" = The Jews

      "all the tribes of the earth" = The Gentiles

      "mourn over Him" They will be sorry to see Him coming. "Even so, Amen"

   3. The Power of the Son 1:8

He is the "Alpha and Omega"

He is the One "Who is, who was, who is to come"

He is the "Almighty"

THE SUBJECT OF THE VISION 1:9-20

I. The Voice John Heard 1:9-11

    A. The Occasion of the Voice 1:9

"John," the fisherman, and apostle. The unified voice of the early church declares John the Apostle as the author of Revelation. Clement of Alexandria, Justin Martyr, Irenaus, Tertullian, Hypolytus, Origen, and Eusebius all attribute the book to him.

"your brother" He does not call Himself an apostle. He's sending a message of encouragement to his brothers.

"fellow partaker" He identifies with those suffering saints.

"tribulation"= "thlipsis" It means suffering. John was not an armchair encourager.

"perseverance"= "hupomone" It means endurance. Not passive submission, but courageous resistance.

"kingdom" This is what makes the suffering worthwhile.

"Patmos" John was banished to this rocky island in the Mediterranean for 2 reasons:

        1. "the word of God" He refused to compromise.

        2. "the testimony of Jesus" He refused to keep quiet.

    B. The Circumstances of the Voice 1:10

"I was in the Spirit on the Lord's day." The Lord's day does not seem to be the "day of the Lord." It refers instead to the day of our Lord's resurrection, Sunday. This was the day set aside by the early church for worship (cf. 1 Cor. 16:1-4). John was in exile and could not attend a worship service. He was still, however, going to worship the Lord, and so he was "in the Spirit." John was worshipping when God spoke to him. That is the way that God speaks to us most often.

    C. The Command of the Voice 1:11

        1. "write...what you see" He is going to see a vision.

        2. "send it to the seven churches" It is a message for the church.

II. The Vision John Saw 1:12-16

Notice twelve observations John makes.

    1. "seven golden lampstands" 1:13 cf.1:20

They are representative of the seven churches of 1:11. They are also representative of all churches in all ages.

Is the lampstand a good symbol of a church? Phil. 2:15

    2. "in the middle of the lampstands" 1:13

He is the Lord of the Lampstands. Jesus has control over those lampstands. He has authority to turn them on or off. He has the responsibility to protect them. He also has a direct relationship to each and every church.

3. "like a son of man" 1:13

Jesus retains a human form. He is eternally the God-man.

4. "robe" 1:13

This word refers to the robe of a high priest, possibly a king or a judge. Jesus is the church's great high priest. He is also the judge of the church. And He will do His job. This refers to His role as the judge of the church.

5. "His head and His hair were white like white wool" 1:14

This refers to His purity. He is a holy priest, and a completely righteous judge (cf. Dan. 7:9 a reference to the "Ancient of Days").

This also refers to His right to judge the church.

6. "His eyes were like a flame of fire" 1:14

This points to the piercing judgment of His eyes. Nothing is hidden from His vision. This refers to His ability to judge the church.

7. "His feet were like burnished bronze" 1:15

This is a reference to the crushing judgment of Christ's feet. Like a worker in a wine vat, He comes to stamp out justice and judgment. He comes to crush the head of the serpent (cf. Gen. 3:15/ Rom. 16:20).

8. "His voice like the sound of many waters." 1:15

This speaks of His authority. There are many voices competing for our attention and allegiance today. His voice alone is authoritative.

9. "His right hand" 1:16

This is the place of honor, protection, and great responsibility.

10. "seven stars" 1:16 cf. 1:20

They are the seven angels of the seven churches. The Greek word "angelos" means "messenger." It could refer to angelic messengers like Gabriel and Michael. It could also refer to human messengers (cf. Luke 9:52, and James 2:25). If it refers to human messengers, then it refers to the pastors of these seven churches. Since they are held in Christ's right hand, the place of great honor, protection, and responsibility, people should be very careful about how they treat these messengers. These messengers should also be very careful how they represent Christ, since He can crush them at any moment.

11. "Out of His mouth came a sharp two-edged sword" 1:16

This "sword" refers to the basis of His judgment, the word of God (cf. Heb. 4:12, Rev. 19:13-15, Eph. 6:17).

12. "His face was like the sun" 1:16

This refers to His overwhelming glory.

III. The Victory John Experienced 1:17-20

A. A Victory over Familiarity 1:17

John fell at Jesus' feet as a dead man. He was overwhelmed by His glory and holiness. How Christians need to learn this lesson today. John had known Jesus personally, but now he falls before Him in awe and respect. We should have the same kind of awe and respect for Him today.

B. A Victory over Fear 1:17-18

1. Jesus offers Words of Comfort. 1:17b "fear not" (cf. 2 Tim. 1:7)

The phrase "fear not" and similar instructions are found 93 times in the Old Testament and 24 times in the New Testament. Jesus used this phrase with Peter, James and John on the Mount of Transfiguration.

2. Jesus offers Words of Confidence. 1:17b-18

a. "I am the first and the last"

His eternal existence is in view here (cf. Psalm 90:2).

b. "and the living one; and I was dead"

This speaks of His redemptive death and His victorious resurrection.

c. "I am alive forevermore"

He is eternally alive and eternally able to save (cf. Heb. 7:25).

d. "I have the keys of death and hades"

Keys are symbols of authority (Matt. 16:19). Jesus Christ has authority over death which claims the body, and hades which claims the soul.

Where will your body and soul spend eternity?

C. A Victory over our Foe. 1:19-20

In these verses Jesus assures John that the ultimate victory is His.

1. Jesus offers Words of Command. 1:19 "write"

In this verse, Jesus commands John to write the book of Revelation and gives the divine outline of the book.

a. "the things which you have seen" Chapter 1

b. "the things which are" Chapters 2-3

c. "the things which shall take place after these things" Chapters 4-22

2. Jesus offers Words of Commentary. 1:20

In this verse Jesus explains the symbols of the "seven stars" (cf. 1:16), and the "seven lampstands" (cf. 1:12). Though the book of Revelation gives many symbols, most of them are explained, or can be explained by using the rest of the Scriptures.

Lose your First Love

LESSON 3
LETTERS TO THE CHURCHES: PART 1
(REVELATION 2:1-29)

A 54c

We are now entering the second great division of the Book of Revelation as found in chapter 1 verse 19. Chapter 1 dealt with the vision of Christ that John saw. Chapters two and three will discuss "the things which are." These are the things of the churches. In chapters two and three, Jesus sends a personal letter to seven churches in Asia Minor, or modern day Turkey. It is important for us to remember that these were all literal congregations of believers in their respective cities. Jesus addresses genuine issues that these congregations were facing. What issues would Jesus raise if He wrote a letter to our church? What issues would He raise if He wrote a personal letter to you? (cf. Appendix 4)

These churches are also representative of the churches of all church history. Each church has its own personality, and peculiarities. Each church of today can find characteristics of itself both positive and negative in these seven churches. Each church has some areas to be praised and some areas to be improved. Use these chapters as a mirror in which you can see yourself and your church.

THE CHURCH OF EPHESUS

Ephesus was the chief city of Asia. It was located on a harbor. It was the center for the worship of "Diana," the goddess of fertility. Her temple was the largest of the ancient world, and considered to be one of the seven wonders of the world. The church was founded by the Apostle Paul on his 3rd missionary journey, and he pastored the church for three years. It was probably during that time that the other six churches were also started. This church was privileged to have been led by some of the greatest men of the New Testament, Paul, John, Apollos, and Timothy.

In each of these letters to the churches, the same pattern is followed: 1) the Lord's Character before His church, 2) The Lord's Commendation for His church, 3) The Lord's Complaint against His church, 4) The Lord's Command for His church, and 5) the Lord's Challenge for His church. This is the pattern that will be followed in this study in all of these letters.

I. The Lord's Character before His Church 2:1

Churches AT A IN city.

9

Each of these letters is addressed to the "angel of the church." These "angels" are mentioned in 1:16, 20 where they are also referred to as "stars." The word "angel" in the Greek literally means "messenger" and can refer to a heavenly messenger which we call an angel, or an earthly messenger like a preacher or pastor. In Luke 7:27 this word is used to refer to John the Baptist.

In this study, we will take it to refer to the earthly messenger of the church, the person that God holds responsible for the doctrine, conduct, and expansion of the church, the pastor.

> "the One who holds the seven stars in His right hand"

> In holding the seven stars Jesus shows His role as protector of the church. He is also the owner of the churches. They are in His right hand.

> "the One who walks among the seven golden lampstands"

> The lampstands are the churches (1:20). Jesus walks among His churches. It is His responsibility to inspect the lamps and do what is necessary to keep them burning. He is the Lord of the churches and the Judge of the churches. We are accountable to Him. He is active, not passive in His responsibility. He is walking, not sitting or standing.

II. The Lord's Commendation for His Church 2:2-3,6

Notice the words "I know." These are very encouraging words. Jesus knows what you have done for Him. He has not overlooked your hard work or your sufferings on His account. Jesus points to 7 positive things in their church.

Pergeas

1. Their deeds = good works

2. Their toil = hard work

3. Their perseverance = endurance

4. They could not endure evil men = intolerance of false teachers

5. They had discernment = They "put to the test"

6. They had not grown weary = They refused to give up

7. They hated the deeds of the Nicolaitans = They opposed the cults.

III. The Lord's Complaint Against His Church 2:4

"you have left your first love"

> They left their first love, they did not lose it. This was a sin of the heart, not the hand. "First love" means "best love." Serving Christ had become a duty instead of a joy. They had lost their intense, enthusiastic devotion for Jesus Christ (cf. John 14:23,/ 21:15-17).

> *Do you have your "first love" for Jesus?*

IV. The Lord's Command for His Church 2:5

A. "Remember"

B. "Repent"

C. "Return"

Love can be lost, but love can be regained.

Warning: "I...will remove your lampstand." The lampstand refers to the church's testimony or influence. Today, Ephesus is only a marsh. There is no church there and no witness within miles.

V. The Lord's Challenge for His Church 2:7

"ear" = spiritual insight or discernment

"let him hear" = Hearing in the Old Testament and New Testament implies more than just physical hearing. It means to hear and obey.

"overcomes" = Overcoming is a theme in all seven letters. It refers to the believer who, by faith, is faithful to do what Jesus commands (cf. 1 John 5:4).

"tree of life" = The tree of life which is lost in Genesis is regained in Revelation.

THE CHURCH OF SMYRNA

Smyrna is the only one of these seven cities still existing today. It is the modern city of Izmer. It was a lovely city and wealthy city full of beautiful buildings. There were two great threats to Christians in Smyrna. Smyrna was a center for Roman Emperor worship. Everyone was asked to bow at an altar and say "Caesar is Lord." There was also a large anti-Christian Jewish population in Smyrna. It was tough being a Christian in Smyrna. It cost something to be a Christian there. Smyrna was the martyr church, a suffering church. Jesus sends them words of encouragement (Barclay, 73-76).

I. The Lord's Character before His Church 2:8

"the first and the last"

This emphasized Jesus' eternality (cf. Psalm 90:2).

"who was dead, and has come to life"

Only Jesus can say this. It refers to His resurrection. This was a word of great encouragement to believers who were risking their lives for Him.

II. The Lord's Commendation for His Church 2:9

"I know" These were words of great comfort to these persecuted saints. He mentions three things in particular.

1. "your tribulation"

2. "your poverty"

3. "the blasphemy" = slander

III. The Lord's Complaint against His Church

There is none. There are only words of comfort and encouragement. Only two churches receive no complaints: Smyrna, the martyr church, and Philadelphia, the evangelistic church.

IV. The Lord's Command for His Church 2:10a

1. "do not fear"

2. "be faithful unto death" cf. Heb. 12:2

V. The Lord's Challenge to His Church 2:10b-11

Jesus offers these faithful believers 2 promises.

1. The crown of life

This reward is for those who endure persecution, (cf. James 1:12/ Matt. 5:10-12, 44).

2. Deliverance from the second death

The first death is physical. The second death is spiritual. The first birth is physical. The second birth is spiritual (John 3:1-7). Revelation 20:13-15 describes the second death. Someone said if you're born once you'll die twice, but if you're born twice, you'll only die once.

Church

All city
Go miles afst

THE CHURCH OF PERGAMUM

Pergamum was an inland city. It was a city of great learning, great temples, and it was the custodian of the old Greek way of life. It was also the administrative center of Asia. The governors of Pergamum had the "right of the sword." This meant that they could execute whom they wished. The saints in Smyrna were faithful in suffering and persecution, the saints in Pergamum were beginning to compromise under persecution (Barclay, 87-90).

PERGAMUM
mox montege

I. The Lord's Character before His Church 2:12

"the One who has the sharp two-edged sword"

Christ says He is the one who carries the sword(1:16/ 19:15,20). He is reminding this church that He is the judge not only of the world, but also of the church. The sword is the word of God(Heb. 4:12,13). The word is an instrument of life and of death. It is capable of dividing truth and error, right and wrong. Jesus does not hold the sword for nothing. He will use it.

II. The Lord's Commendation for His Church 2:13

A. They are commended for staying in a tough place. "where Satan's throne is"

Satan does not live in hell, he rules on earth. He is called the "god of this world" (2 Cor. 4:4). Pergamum was a city of great idolatry with temples to Zeus, Athena, Dionysus, and Asclepius. It is amazing that these Christians chose to stay in such a city in spite of the persecution. Christians need to serve the Lord even where it is tough.

B. They are commended for being identified with Jesus.

"you hold fast My name" They didn't mind being called Christians.

"and did not deny my faith" They continued to hold to the authority and inerrancy of the Scripture. They did this even when "Antipas", probably their pastor, was executed for being a Christian.

III. The Lord's Complaint against His Church 2:14-15

The problem with the church at Pergamum was that they tolerated false teaching and this led to loose living. What you believe is important.

A. The teaching of Balaam *Bad*

Back in the book of Numbers (22-25), Balaam was a false prophet who prophesied for whomever paid the most. He showed King Balak that he could use Moabite women to seduce the men of Israel into sexual immorality, idolatry, and intermarriage. Apparently there were some people teaching in their church that it was OK to intermarry with pagans, attend idolatrous worship, and continue to go to the Temple prostitutes.

B. The teaching of the Nicolaitans *Jude 11 II Peter 2-15*

Most commentators believe this was an early church cult that abused their freedom. They apparently taught that since they were saved and forgiven then they could live any old way. Of course, many lived this way to save themselves trouble and persecution. Not only did they have members who lived this way, they had teachers in their church who taught this way. Revelation 2:6 said that God hated the deeds of the Nicolaitans.

IV. The Lord's Command to His Church 2:16 *Act 8-4*

"repent...or else"

The church was told to deal with these false teachers or Jesus would bring His sword and make war with them personally. There are two ways to deal with moral compromise in the church: repentance, or judgment. Jesus is not bluffing.

V. The Lord's Challenge to His Church 2:17

It is a message of hope, not condemnation. If they will "hear" and obey the message, in other words "repent," then Jesus promised to reward them in three ways:

A. "I will give some of the hidden manna"

A promise of spiritual food to sustain the believer in the most difficult times. Perhaps also a promise of material sustenance during their persecution.

B. "I will give him a white stone"

Jurors cast their votes by means of a black stone for guilt and a white stone for innocence. This is Christ's personal promise for forgiveness and restoration.

C. "a new name written on the stone"

A promise of a new beginning and a new character, a clean slate. A church or an individual Christian can start over. This is a great promise.

4-3-2016

THE CHURCH OF THYATIRA *Good church*

Of all the cities in which these seven churches were located, Thyatira was the smallest, least known, and least remarkable. It was a small town compared to Ephesus and the church shouldn't compare itself to FBC Ephesus. It was a military outpost founded to be a buffer zone for Pergamum to slow down invading armies. It was expendable. It was a small town, rural, middle class, hard working community (Barclay, 101,102). Jesus sends a letter here to encourage believers who live and minister in small places, and to remind us that big problems can exist in small towns and small churches (Swindoll, 26).

I. The Lord's Character before His Church 2:18

    A. "The Son of God"   This is a strong claim of His deity.

    B. "who has eyes like a flame of fire"   cf. 1:14

    C. "His feet are like burnished bronze" cf. 1:15

Rev 2 - 23
11   18
19
2 - 21 - 23
2 - 24 25

II. The Lord's Commendation to His Church 2:19

    A. "deeds"   They were an active church.

    B. "love"   They were a loving church, the opposite of Ephesus.

    C. "faith"   They were willing to step out on faith and take a risk.

    D. "service"   The members were involved in serving the Lord and His Church.

    E. "perseverance"   They endured during the tough times. They didn't quit.

    F. "your deeds of late are greater than at the first"   They were progressive, just the opposite of Ephesus.

III. The Lord's Complaint against His Church 2:20-23

This church did not face an external threat, but an internal threat that, if ignored, could destroy the church.

    A. Toleration of false doctrine

What you believe is important. False doctrine always leads to false practice.

    B. Toleration of a false teacher

"the woman Jezebel who calls herself a prophetess"

2 - 20 The Old Testament queen named Jezebel led Israel into a false system of worship that involved idolatry and immorality. This woman was probably a gifted teacher that taught it was alright for the Christians to participate in the feasts that were given to honor their pagan idols. There was usually much drinking and immorality associated with these feasts.

    C. A promise of judgment for the false teacher and her followers

Her false teaching concerning idolatry was compared to adultery ("immorality" 2:21). Going after false gods is spiritual adultery. She had already refused to repent (2:21), but her followers were given time to "repent." "Children" in verse 23 refers to those who followed her teaching.

IV. The Lord's Command to His Church 2:24-25

    A. To Jezebel's followers   "repent" v.22

    B. To the rest of the church   "what you have hold fast" v. 25

"deep things of Satan"

"until I come"   Notice His promise to come.

Jezebel died 1000 year when Christ came on the scene

14

V. The Lord's Challenge for His Church 2:26-29

There are two promises made to those who overcome and are obedient:

1. "I will give authority over the nations"   cf. Psalm 2:8

There will be ruling responsibilities for faithful Christians in Christ's kingdom.

2. "I will give him the morning star"   cf. Rev. 22:16

This pictures Christ in His role as the One who gives illumination. How wonderful for a Christian to have constant fellowship with the One who provides this illumination.

54 in All
7 ages in Historic
R. 2 - 1 = 2-2
   angle
c 2 - 1

II   2-2-3
      Save by Grace Not by works - .

2 c Acts

Rev - 2- 19

EpH - 1 - 4
Titus 2 - 14

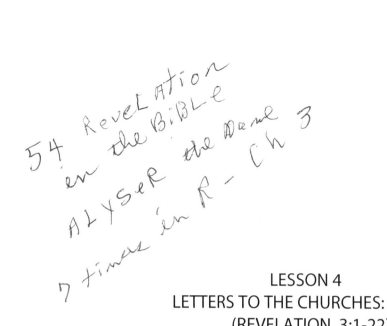

54   Revelation in the Bible
ALYSeR the Name
7 times in R - Ch 3

I Peter 1 - 15

LESSON 4
LETTERS TO THE CHURCHES: PART 2
(REVELATION 3:1-22)

THE CHURCH OF SARDIS

The city of Sardis had a reputation for having an attitude of smugness and sleepiness. Their city was built on a hill and they felt they were impregnable. They felt so safe they refused to post guards. They had been conquered by both the Persians and the Greeks because they were asleep when the enemy arrived. Like many Christians, they were sleeping when they should have been awake, resting when they should have been fighting. The attitude within the city had also invaded the church. They were also sleeping when they should have been alert to spiritual danger (Barclay, 113-116).

Holie owl

I. The Lord's Character before His Church 3:1

    A. He is all <u>wise</u>. "He who has the seven spirits"

He is all wise. He has the fullness of the Spirit.

    B. He is <u>sovereign</u>. "and the seven stars"

He has the seven stars in His sovereign possession. He still has His messengers in the world.

II. The Lord's <u>Commendation</u> for His Church

There is not one word of commendation for this once great church. They had a reputation for being alive, but they were <u>dead</u>. They were active, but doing what? They had at one time been a loving, and faithful church, but no more. They became <u>complacent</u>, satisfied, comfortable, and <u>lazy</u>.

III. The Lord's <u>Complaint</u> against His Church 3:1-2

He has very little in the way of specific complaints against them. They were asleep and needed to wake up and they were <u>weak</u> and needed to be strengthened(v.2). He also says that their deeds were not <u>complete</u> before God(v.2). Perhaps they felt that they had arrived and were doing well. It is interesting that Jesus does not complain about false teaching. Apparently they were not active enough in Bible study to even have any false doctrine. He doesn't mention any persecution. They were so lifeless and powerless they weren't experiencing any persecution. They were harmless in the eyes of the world.

IV. The Lord's Command to His Church 3:2-3

A. "Wake up"

They had been lulled to sleep. They needed to snap out of their lethargy.

B. "Strengthen the things that remain"

They needed to take inventory and stop losing ground. Every church and every Christian needs to do some introspection and evaluation from time to time.

C. "Remember"

They had forgotten the gospel. They had forgotten what it was like to be lost. They had forgotten the price Jesus paid for them.

Jesus open door & closed door

D. "Keep it"

It is time to be faithful, not fickle.

E. "Repent"

The tense here indicates a one time decisive action. They needed to rededicate themselves to Christ. There were some things that needed to change.

V. The Lord's Challenge to His Church 3:4-6

A. A message to the faithful few.

Revival always begins with just a few. Not everyone in the church was careless about spiritual things. Some were very concerned.

B. Assurance of eternal life.

1. "clothed in white garments"

They would receive the righteousness of Christ.

2. "name in the book of life"

Their names will be remembered by God (cf. Rev. 20:12-15).

3. "confess his name before My Father"

They will receive God's commendation (cf. Matt. 10:32-33).

THE CHURCH OF PHILADELPHIA

Philadelphia means "brotherly love." It was the youngest of the seven cities. It was located where the borders of Mysia, Lydia, and Phrygia met. It was the doorway to the East. This city was founded by the Greeks for a very specific purpose, that it might spread the Greek culture and language to Lydia and Phrygia. It did its job so well that by 19 a.d., the Lydians had forgotten their own language and were for all purposes Greeks. They had been given an "open door" to spread Greek ideas and now 3 centuries later, they are given another "open door" to spread the gospel (Barclay, 125-127).

I. The Lord's <u>Character</u> Before His Church 3:7

    A. <u>Holy</u> "He who is holy"

He is <u>set apart</u> from creation. He is completely <u>separate</u> from sin (cf. 1 Pet. 2:21-22, and 1:14-16).

    B. <u>True</u> "who is true"

"True" here means <u>genuine</u>, <u>real</u>. He is the One and Only. He is the authentic way to God (cf. John 14:6).

    C. <u>Sovereign</u> "who has the key of David"

Keys are important. <u>Keys</u> show <u>authority</u> and <u>responsibility</u>. Since He holds the key, He can open the door.

II. The Lord's <u>Commendation</u> to His Church 3:8-10

    A. Commended

        1. "you have a little power"

They used <u>all</u> God had given them.

        2. "you...have kept my word"

They <u>believed</u> God's word and <u>practiced</u> it.

        3. "you...have not denied My name"

They remained <u>faithful</u> in spite of <u>opposition</u>.

    B. Rewarded

"I have put before you an open door which no one can shut"

Sometimes the reward for serving Christ is greater responsibility (cf. 1 Cor. 16:8-9/ 2 Cor. 2:12).

The "open door" is the door of evangelistic opportunity (cf. Acts 14:27).

    C. Encouraged

        1. <u>Vindication</u> <u>v. 9</u>

Their enemies will "bow down" (cf. Joseph and his brothers, Gen. 42:6).

        2. <u>Deliverance</u> v.10

"I will keep you from the hour of testing."

This seems to be a reference to the *Pre-tribulation Rapture*. God never promises to keep the church from <u>testing and tribulation</u>. In fact He promises we will have tribulation in this world (John 16:33). But Jesus does promise that the Church will *not* have to face His wrath or this "hour of testing, that is about to come upon the whole world." "Hour of testing" refers to a <u>specified</u> <u>period</u> of time. "Whole world" indicates that this will be a <u>worldwide</u> judgment, like the Tribulation. The preposition "from" means "<u>out of</u>." God promises to keep His church "out of" the Tribulation period, *not* keep the church "through" it (cf. Matt. 24:14-21/ 1 Thess. 1:10/ 4:17/ 5:9). (cf. Appendix 1)

III. The Lord's Complaint against His Church

There is no complaint against this church. They have been doing the best they can. There is no complaint against Smyrna, the Persecuted Church. And there is no complaint against Philadelphia, the Evangelistic Church.

IV. The Lord's Command to His Church 3:11

Power of the Air

A. A Word of Counsel

"I am coming quickly"

"Quickly" refers to the manner of His coming. It will be sudden.

His coming is a warning to the careless, and a comfort to the committed.

church
6 1-4
church is
in Heaven

B. A Word of Command

"Hold fast what you have"

He is saying: Don't back up. Don't slow down. Don't let up. Complete your task. Accept the Challenge. Walk through the door.

Jesus come Back
Befor the Rapture

C. A Word of Caution

"In order that no one take your crown"

The "crown" refers to "eternal rewards," *not* "eternal life." It is possible for us to lose our rewards and others gain what we could have had if we had been obedient to Christ.

V. The Lord's Challenge to His Church 3:12-13

Two promises are made to those who walk through doors that Jesus opens:

1. "I will make him a pillar in the temple of My God."

Special citizens had a pillar placed in the temple with their name on it. This refers to a place of security and honor in Heaven.

2. "I will write upon him the name..."

This is a promise of 3 new names. A name is a mark of ownership and identification with Christ. At adoption people were given a new name.

R - 3-10

THE CHURCH OF LAODICEA

Laodicea was a located on the most important trade route in Asia. It was a major center for the textile industry and the clothing industry. Laodicea also had one of the most important medical centers of its day. It particularly specialized in eyesalves. It was world renowned for its eyesalves (Barclay, 137-139).

I. The Lord's Character before His Church 3:14

7 Church
7 - Letter

Re 3-14

19

A. "The Amen"

This expression is usually used at the end of a sentence to guarantee its truthfulness. Jesus' promises are utterly reliable.

B. "The faithful and true witness"

Jesus was an authentic witness for the Father (cf.John 1:18).

C. "The beginning of the creation of God"

cf. John 1:1-3/ Col. 1:16

II. The Lord's Commendation for His Church

There is no word of commendation for this backslidden church.

III. The Lord's Complaint against His Church 3:15-18

A. Their Lukewarmness 3:15-16

Laodicea was known for its lukewarm water. The people in the church were not bad people. They were just *not* spiritual people. They were indifferent to the things of God. They were complacent, lethargic, and apathetic. Their spiritual apathy made Jesus sick.

B. Their Pride 3:17-18   *Rich*

Their strengths became their weaknesses. They were self deceived into thinking that they could get by without God. They thought they had "need of nothing." That is spiritual pride and there are many churches and many Christians that have that very same attitude today.

They said:	God said:
We are rich.	You are poor.
We can see.	You are blind.
We are well dressed.	You are naked.

truth of God

R-3-20

IV. The Lord's Command for His Church 3:19-20

A. His Love for the Church 3:19

"Those whom I love, I reprove and discipline"

Jesus is not finished with them yet. He still loves them. He still disciplines them. He still loves the backslidden church and believer.

B. His Command for the Church 3:19

"Be zealous therefore, and repent"

The word "zealous" means "boiling." Jesus means for them to repent quickly and enthusiastically.

C. His Invitation to the Church 3:20

This is an invitation to churches that have departed from New Testament Christianity. It is also an invitation to individuals who claim to be Christians and may even be church members, but have never truly been born again.

"I"=Jesus Christ

"door"=the entrance to a person's life (or a church's life)

"knock"=Jesus seeks entrance by knocking. He will *not* force His way.

"anyone"=This promise is large enough to include *any* individual.

"open"=The door is opened by trusting in Christ (cf. Acts 16:31/ Eph. 2:8-9).

"For whoever will call upon the name of the Lord will be saved." Rom. 10:13

Have you personally opened the door of your life to Jesus?

"I will come in"=This a two-fold <u>promise</u> of salvation and fellowship.

V. The Lord's <u>Challenge</u> for His Church 3:21-22

"I will grant to him to sit down on my throne"

This is a promise that not only will we be on the winning side, but we will be <u>ruling</u> and reigning with Christ (cf. Matt. 19:28/ 2 Tim. 2:12/ Rev. 20:4).

Conclusion: *Jesus is the Amen for God*

Jesus Christ is the Lord of the Church and He will evaluate each church according to its faithfulness to Him, to the truth, and to its task of evangelizing the world. He also evaluates individuals inside and outside of the church. *Zeal for Jesus*

In Revelation 3:20 we read a wonderful invitation that is open to any individual who would like to have a personal relationship with Jesus Christ, and have their sins forgiven forever. "Behold, I stand at the door and knock, if *anyone* hears My voice and opens the door, *I will come in* to him, and will dine with <u>him, and he with Me</u>. Perhaps you have never personally accepted Jesus' <u>invitation to come into your life and save you</u>, but you would really like to know that He is in your life. That is why He died on the cross for our sins, so we could have them forgiven and have a personal relationship with Him. If you would like for the Lord Jesus to come into your life right now, you can "open" the door of your life by praying this simple prayer:

Dear Lord Jesus, Thank you for loving me and dying on the cross for all my sins. Please come into my life right now and save me. Forgive me of all my sin. Make me a part of your family. Give me a home in Heaven someday. I trust you alone to be my Savior right now. I accept your gracious invitation, and I am claiming your promise to "come in" right now.   Amen.

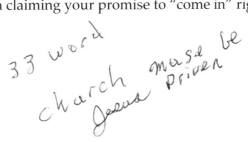

33 word
church must be
Jesus proven

LESSON 5
THE THRONE ROOM OF HEAVEN
(REVELATION 4:1-11)

[handwritten: Ch church Not Her is gone]

Introduction:

Revelation chapter 4 begins the third and final major division of the book based on the outline found in 1:19. From this point on everything in the book refers to future things. This section will describe the terrible judgments of the Great Tribulation, especially chapters 6-19. Before John describes the events of the Tribulation for us, he gives us a glimpse into the throne room of Heaven in chapters 4 and 5. Before the Tribulation begins there is a grand event planned for all Christians. It is the Rapture of the Church and it is pictured in the opening verses of chapter 4.

THE INVITATION TO HEAVEN 4:1-3

[handwritten: 7 years Hell on Earth]

I. A Depiction of the Rapture 4:1-3 (John's experience)

Although we are not told this is the "rapture," it certainly pictures it very accurately. It takes place before the judgments of the Tribulation are unleashed and the word "church" is not mentioned again in the discussion concerning the Tribulation. This is a reason that many scholars believe in a *"Pre-Tribulation Rapture."*

A. "After these things" 4:1

This is the very first phrase in the original text. This is identical to the Greek phrase, "meta tauta," found in 1:19 where we find John's outline for the book. After what things? The things of the *churches* found in chapters 2-3.

B. "A door standing open in heaven" 4:1

There are four doors in Revelation (Revelation, Ryrie, 38).

   1. Rev. 3:8 The door of opportunity

   2. Rev. 3:20 The door to your life

3. Rev. 4:1 An open door to <u>heaven</u> for the Christian

open door

4. Rev. 19:11 The door through which <u>Jesus</u> <u>comes</u> to judge the earth.

The door to heaven is standing open today. Jesus is that door (John 10:9/ 14:6).

Have you personally entered by faith through Him for salvation?   *in Heaven*

C. "The voice"   4:1

The voice of the glorified Christ from 1:10. It sounded like a "<u>trumpet</u>." This is another depiction of the Rapture when we are told the "trumpet will sound" (cf. 1 Thess. 4:16/ 1 Cor. 15:52).

D. "Come up here"   4:1

The scene now shifts from <u>earth</u> to <u>heaven</u>. This depicts the rapture because the call to John is to come up to heaven. Notice that it occurs <u>before</u> the Tribulation begins.

E. "Immediately"   4:2

He was in heaven "at once." There was no waiting. This is a depiction of the rapture because the rapture will be a <u>sudden</u> event. cf. 1 Cor. 15:52

II. A <u>Description</u> of the Rapture   (Our Experience)

4 John when ✝ Heaven

A. What is the Rapture?

1. The <u>word</u>

Latin= "rapturo" It means to "seize" or "snatch."

Greek= "harpazo" It means to "snatch" or "take away" (cf.Acts 8:39/ 2 Cor. 12:2-4/ 1 Thess. 4:17).

2. The <u>event</u>

"Rapture" is an umbrella word to describe several events.

a. a <u>return</u>   1 Thess. 4:16

b. a <u>resurrection</u>   1 Thess 4:16/ 1 Cor. 15:52

c. a <u>rapture</u>   1 Thess 4:17

d. a <u>reunion</u>   1 Thess. 4:17 (<u>Basic Theology</u>, Ryrie, 462-463)

B. When is the Rapture?

Revelation 6-19 describes a <u>seven</u> year period known as the Tribulation. There are at least three views as to when the Rapture will be. (cf. Appendix 5)

1. <u>Post</u>-Tribulation view.

The Rapture occurs <u>after</u> the Tribulation.

2. <u>Mid</u>-Tribulation view.

The Rapture occurs at the <u>mid-point</u> of the Tribulation.

3. <u>Pre</u>-Tribulation view.

The Rapture occurs just <u>before</u> the Tribulation.

Four reasons for a Pre-Tribulational view:

1. The promise to the church at Philadelphia (Rev. 3:10).
2. The promises that the church will not have to endure God's wrath which is what the Tribulation is (1 Thess. 1:10/ 5:9/ Rev. 6:16-17).
3. The "church" is mentioned often in Revelation before chapter 4, but it is not mentioned even once in chapters 4-19 which discuss the events of the Tribulation. The "church" will apparently not be on earth during the Tribulation.
4. Jesus' coming for His church is pictured in the New Testament as imminent (Matt. 24:36,42,44).

C. How soon is the Rapture?

Soon. There is no sign that must be performed before He comes. There is no prophecy that must be fulfilled before He comes.

If He comes today, are you prepared?

THE ADORATION IN HEAVEN   4:3-11

live with God for every [handwritten]

I. The Person Seated on the Throne   4:1-3

   A. The Throne   4:2-3

"Throne" is mentioned 45 times in Revelation, only 15 times in the rest of the New Testament. It is used to stress the sovereignty of God. This is a throne of judgment. (cf. Heb. 4:16 for a throne of grace.) The rainbow surrounding the throne is a vivid reminder of the faithfulness of God (cf. Gen. 9:13).

   B. The Person   4:2-3

It is God the Father (cf. 4:8). We also see the Holy Spirit in the picture in Revelation 4:5. In chapter 5 and verse 6 we see God the Son.

II. The People Surrounding the Throne   4:4-7

   A. The 24 elders   4:4

Some see them as angels though they probably represent saved humanity. They don't seem to be angels since they are wearing crowns and seated on thrones. The white garments they wear speak eloquently of the righteousness of Christ (Wiersbe, 582).

   B. The 4 living creatures   4:6-7

They are angelic beings which represent each realm of creation (cf. Isa. 6:1-3/ Gen 9:10 God's covenant with Noah).

III. The Praise Swelling to the Throne   4:8-11

   A. From the Living Creatures   4:8-9

They are praising the Almighty.

4-9-11

B. From the 24 Elders   4:10-11

They are praising the Creator.

In chapter 4 they praise God for His great work of creation. In chapter 5 they will praise God for His great work of redemption.

4 - 11

R - 5 - 8 - 9

R 3 = 18
    2 = 10
R 4 = 1 - 6

R 6 - 1

54 seven of Revelation

LESSON 6
THE WORSHIP OF HEAVEN
(REVELATION 5:1-14)

The scene in Revelation chapter 5 is still in Heaven. It is a continuation of chapter 4. Chronologically, this chapter precedes the horrible "seal" judgments of chapter 6. Heaven is preparing itself for the judgments that are coming. The world is continuing its pattern of wickedness and independence from God. This chapter answers the question "Who is worthy to judge the earth?" It helped those early Christians to know that there would come a time of reckoning for this world that had so persecuted them. This chapter also includes a high moment of praise and worship in the heavenlies that all Christians will have the privilege of participating in someday. The book that is mentioned is actually a scroll of redemption and judgment that cannot be opened and executed by just anyone.

THE ONE WE WORSHIP 5:1-7

I. The Scroll of <u>Redemption</u> 5:1

   A. The <u>Position</u> of the Scroll

   "in the right hand of Him who sat on the throne"

   This is a reference to God the Father.

   B. The <u>Description</u> of the Scroll

   It is a scroll. It is *not* a book. It is <u>rolled</u>. It is "written inside and on the back." Nothing could be added. It was complete and full. It was "sealed with seven seals" like a Roman will. This scroll of redemption and <u>judgment</u> must be unrolled little by little as each seal is broken. The contents of the scroll were revealed to John and are found in the judgments executed in chapters 6-19.

   C. The <u>Definition</u> of the Scroll

   Someone has called it the <u>title</u> <u>deed</u> to the earth, the title deed to all that God promised Christ for His sacrifice (Ps. 2:8). The subject of the scroll is redemption. Redemption has its roots in the past, but its ultimate fulfillment lies in the future (Lk 21:28/Rom. 8:22-23). In ancient times, a title deed could only be opened by the appointed heir (Wiersbe, 584). Jesus is God's appointed heir (cf. Heb. 1:2). God created Adam and gave him dominion, but Adam sinned. A usurper is now trying to run things, but Jesus will ultimately be victorious.

II. The Search for a <u>Redeemer</u> 5:2-4

The "strong angel" who makes search throughout heaven for a redeemer may be Gabriel whose name means "the mighty one of God."

    A. The <u>Requirement</u> of the Search   5:2

The question was "Who is *worthy* to open the book and to break its seals?" In other words "Who has the <u>right</u> to the title deed of this earth?" "Who is *worthy* to establish justice and righteousness?" Many are <u>willing</u> to try, but who is *worthy*?

    B. The <u>Result</u> of the Search   5:3

"No one" was found. "Heaven" is the <u>angelic</u> realm. "Earth" is the realm of <u>mankind</u>. "Under the earth" is the realm of the <u>demonic</u>, and the accursed dead.

    C. John's <u>Response</u> to the Search   5:4

His response was one of great sorrow ("weep greatly"). He was sorrowful because it seemed that in and suffering on the earth must <u>continue</u>. God's glorious plan of redemption and salvation could never be completed until the scroll was opened. There seemed to be no one who was worthy to judge sin and put an end to sin and suffering. Not even God the Father, since He is not a man can do this (John 5:22).

III. The Selection of the <u>Redeemer</u>   5:5-7

John heard a voice that interrupted his weeping with a message of hope. Someone is worthy. He is sinless humanity.

    A. The <u>Lion</u> of the Tribe of Judah   5:5

"Lion"- represents dignity, courage, <u>royalty</u>

"Judah"- Jacob prophesied on his deathbed that the scepter would not depart from the tribe of Judah (cf. Gen 49:9-10).

"Root of David"- He fulfills the <u>prophecies</u> concerning David and will occupy David's throne (cf. 2 Sam. 7:4-17).

    B. The <u>Lamb</u>   5:6-7

John turned expecting to see a fierce <u>lion</u> and saw a <u>lamb</u> instead. Jesus is called "the lamb" 28 times in the book of Revelation (cf. 6:16/ 7:14/ 19:7/ 21:9). The theme of a sacrificial lamb is used throughout Scripture (eg. Passover, Day of Atonement, Isaac's question in Gen. 22:7, John the Baptist's statement in John 1:29, the song of the redeemed in   Rev. 5:12, etc.). This is no ordinary lamb.

        1. "standing as if slain"   <u>resurrected</u>

        2. "seven horns"   <u>all-powerful</u>

        3. "seven eyes"   <u>all-knowing</u>

        4. "seven Spirits of God"   in the <u>fullness</u> of the <u>Spirit</u>

"He took" the book (v.7). This is the most climactic act in all of history. It assures the regaining of all that was lost in Adam's fall.

THE WAY WE WORSHIP 5:8-14

A. W. Tozer said "Worship is the missing jewel of the evangelical church." The word "worship" comes from the English word "worthship." When we worship God we are declaring *His* worth. When we fail to worship God we are also making a statement about what we think of His worth. God is seeking worshippers today (John 4:23-24).

I. Worship is Thanking God for What He's Done. 5:8-10

Worship breaks out in Heaven when the Son of God takes the book of judgment in His hand. He is worthy to judge because He was able to redeem.

    A. The Worshippers   5:8

        1. The four living creatures   =   angelic beings

        2. The 24 elders   =   redeemed humanity

    B. The Elements of Their Worship   5:8-10

        1. Physical action   "fell down"

        2. Musical accompaniment   "harp"

        3. Prayer   "golden bowls full of incense, which are the prayers of the saints"

        4. Inspired Singing   "they sang a new song"

    Chapter four is the old song of creation. Chapter five is the new song of redemption. Their song is found in verses 9 and 10 and worships Jesus for:

        a. His substitutionary death,

        b. His blood shed for all mankind,

        c. His work in making us a kingdom of priests, and

        d. His future reign.

II. Worship is Ascribing to God the Glory for Who He Is. 5:11-14

The hymn in verse 12 involves the 24 elders, the 4 living creatures, and an angelic choir. This is a hymn of worship for Jesus and ascribes to Him 7 rights of sovereignty.

    A. Hymn of Worship to Jesus 5:12

        1. Power   He was born to a peasant family.

        2. Riches   "for your sakes He became poor" (2 Cor. 8:9)

        3. Wisdom   He is the wisdom of God (1 Cor. 1:23-24).

        4. Might   He once shared the weakness of humanity (Phil. 2:7).

        5. Honor   On earth He was dishonored (cf. John 8:49).

6. <u>Glory</u>   On earth He was mocked (cf. Isa. 53:3).

7. Blessing   He became a curse for us (Gal. 3:13).

B. Hymn of Worship to the <u>Father</u> and the <u>Son</u>   5:13-14

This hymn ascends from "every created thing." This may well include redeemed and unredeemed humanity (cf. Phil. 2:9-10).

1. Blessing

2. <u>Honor</u>

3. <u>Glory</u>

4. <u>Dominion</u>   This means the right to rule.

5. <u>Forever</u> and <u>ever</u>

The response of the 4 living creatures is "Amen." The response of the 24 elders is that they "fell down and worshipped."

What is your response to Jesus today? Will you choose to worship Him?

LESSON 7
THE UNVEILING OF ANTI-CHRIST
(REVELATION 6:1-2)

Revelation chapter 6 begins a discussion of a period of future history commonly known as the <u>Tribulation</u> or the <u>Great Tribulation</u>. The material found between chapter 6 and chapter 19 discusses this period of time. It is a <u>seven</u> year period that will be like nothing the earth has ever endured. This time will be marked by *no* Christian compassion. Harold Willmington in his book <u>The King is Coming</u> (pp.59-60.) lists 12 different names that the Bible gives for the Tribulation:

1. The day of the <u>Lord</u> 1 Cor. 1:8, 5:5, Phil. 1:6, 2:16

2. The day of <u>God's</u> vengeance Isa. 34:8

3. The time of <u>Jacob's</u> trouble Jer. 30:7

4. The <u>seventieth</u> week Dan. 9:24-27

5. The great day of his <u>wrath</u> Rev. 6:17

6. The hour of his <u>judgment</u> Rev. 14:7

7. The end of this <u>world</u> Matt. 13:40,49

8. The time of the <u>end</u> Dan. 12:9

9. The <u>indignation</u> Isa. 26:20, 34:2

10. The overspreading of <u>abominations</u> Dan. 9:27

11. The time of <u>trouble</u> such as never was   Dan. 12:1

12. The <u>tribulation</u> Matt. 24:21,29

We are living very close to the beginning of this time. The chronological outline of this material in Revelation 6-19 is found in a series of judgments. In chapter 6 there are a series of seven "<u>seal</u>" judgments. These are followed by seven "<u>trumpet</u>" judgments in chapters 8 and 9. These are followed by seven "<u>bowl</u>" judgments in chapters 15 and 16. Everything else that falls between chapters 6 and 19 is happening <u>during</u> the time of these judgments.

This world is being prepared for this time of judgment even now. Even now the seeds are being sown for a hellish harvest. The world scene causes us to believe it is near. There are tremendous changes going on in <u>Europe</u> that could unite them into one economy and even one military power. The rising power of the <u>Arab</u> states is a sign of the times. The re-emergence of <u>Israel</u> as a world power after 1900 years is a definite sign that His coming is near. The moral, spiritual, and intellectual bankruptcy of our times is frightening. There are problems for which mankind simply does not have the answers. When the Anti-Christ comes, he represents all of those "anti-Christian ideologies that prepare men's minds for the devil's gospel and the ultimate reception of the strong delusion, the great lie (2 Thes. 2:3-12)," (John Phillips, <u>Revelation</u>, 97, 98). The spread of Humanistic philosophy in the western world which emphasizes, evolution, situation ethics, moral freedom, self-sufficiency, sexual permissiveness, anti-religious bias, socialism, one world government, death education, and human destiny, are all planks in the Anti-Christ's platform.

In chapter 6 the seven seals are opened one by one. The first four seals are commonly referred to as the four <u>horsemen</u> of the apocalypse. There is a <u>white</u> horse, a <u>red</u> horse, a <u>black</u> horse, and a <u>pale</u> horse. Today we will focus on the first horse and its rider.

I. The Rider's <u>Identity</u> 6:1-2

  A. His <u>horse</u> 6:2

  This rider has a <u>white</u> horse, but he is not to be confused with the rider in 19:11-16 which is Jesus Christ. Both riders ride <u>white</u> horses and wear <u>crowns</u>, but they are not the same. Their crowns are not the same. In Revelation 19:11-16 Jesus wears a crown that is a "diadem" and is only worn by sovereignty. The crown which is mentioned in 6:2 is a "stephanos" which is worn by a victor. This is the great pretender. He is the <u>counterfeit</u> Christ. He preaches a counterfeit gospel. He is mentioned throughout the Bible.

  Harold Willmington (Willmington, 78) lists six names given to him in the Scriptures other than Anti-Christ (1 John 2:18).

   1. The man of <u>sin</u> 2 Thess. 2:3

   2. The <u>son</u> of perdition 2 Thess. 2:3

   3. The <u>wicked</u> one 2 Thess. 2:8

   4. The willful <u>king</u> Dan. 11:36

   5. The <u>beast</u> Rev. 11:7 (used 36 times in Revelation)

   6. The little <u>horn</u> Dan. 7:8

  B. His <u>equipment</u> 6:2

   1. "a <u>bow</u>"

   This indicates that he comes to make war. He comes with military might.

   2. "a <u>crown</u> was given to him"

   This indicates that his <u>military</u> campaign was successful. He is given a "stephanos," a victor's crown. He establishes an empire through military might. It is interesting that we are not told how he is dressed. There is no indication given that He is the Christ. He is just portrayed as a military leader.

II. The Rider's <u>Activity</u>   6:2

This rider goes out "conquering, and to conquer." In other words, the Anti-Christ is unveiled at the <u>beginning</u> of the Tribulation and his activity is that of consolidating power through <u>military</u> campaign. Like the great leaders of world empires before him, Nebuchadnezzar, Cyrus, Alexander, Caesar, and others, he will be a capable and ruthless military leader. He is described throughout the Bible.

    A. His <u>characteristics</u> (Willmington, 77-78)

        1. An <u>intellectual</u> genius Dan. 8:23

        2. An <u>oratorical</u> genius   Dan. 11:36

        3. A <u>political</u> genius Rev. 17:11,12

        4. A <u>commercial</u> genius   Rev. 13:16,17/ Dan. 11:43

        5. A <u>military</u> genius Rev. 6:2/ 13:4

        6. A <u>religious</u> genius   Rev. 13:8/ 2 Thess. 2:4

    B. His <u>Activities</u> (Willmington, 82)

        1. He begins by controlling the <u>western</u> block.   Rev. 17:12

        2. He makes a 7 year contract with <u>Israel</u> but breaks after 3 1/2 years.   Dan. 9:27

        3. He gains absolute control of the Middle East after the <u>Russian</u> invasion.   Ezek. 38, 39

        4. He attempts to destroy all of <u>Israel</u>.   Rev. 12

        5. He destroys the false <u>religious</u> system, so it will not hinder him.   Rev. 17:16,17

        6. He sets himself up as <u>God</u> to be worshiped.   Dan. 11:36, 37/ 2 Thess. 2:4,11/ Rev. 13:5

        7. He briefly rules over all <u>nations</u>.   Ps. 2/ Dan. 11:36/ Rev. 13:16

        8. He is utterly crushed by the Lord Jesus Christ at the battle of <u>Armageddon</u>.   Rev. 19

        9. He is the first creature to be thrown into the Lake of <u>Fire</u>.   Rev. 19:20

The Anti-Christ will get his power from <u>Satan</u> (Rev. 13:1-4). The world will applaud him as a great leader and peacemaker. They will believe they are entering the <u>Millennium</u>, when they are actually entering the <u>Tribulation</u>. The reason people will so readily believe this is found in 2 Thess. 2:1-12. They will believe the great lie. Since they refuse to believe God's <u>truth</u>, they will fall for the Devil's <u>lie</u>.

Have you fallen for the Devil's lie?

LESSON 8
OPENING THE SEVEN SEALS
(REVELATION 6:1-17)

Revelation chapters 6 through 19 discuss the <u>events</u> and <u>characters</u> of the Tribulation. Why should there ever be the need for such a terrible time of judgment? Harold Willmington in his book <u>The King is Coming</u>, lists 6 reasons for this judgment (Willmington, 70-74).

1. To <u>harvest</u> the crop that has been sown throughout the ages by God, Satan, and mankind.

2. To prove the falseness of the Devil's <u>claim</u> (Isa. 14:12-14).

3. To prepare a great martyred multitude for <u>heaven</u> (Rev. 7:9, 14).

4. To prepare a great living multitude for the <u>millennium</u> (Matt. 25:32-34).

5. To <u>punish</u> the Gentiles (Rom. 1:18/ 2 Thess. 2:11-12/ Rev. 19:15).

6. To <u>purge</u> Israel (Ezek. 20:37-38/ Zech. 13:8-9/ Mal. 3:3).

The seven seals are the opening events of the Tribulation period. They are a necessary part of Christ claiming the title deed to the planet.

I. The First Seal: World <u>Domination</u> 6:1-2

We've already discussed this first seal as the unveiling of Anti-Christ. It is a world conqueror on a <u>white</u> horse. The "bow" speaks of <u>war</u>. The "crown" speaks of <u>victory</u>. "Conquering and to conquer" speaks of his motivation as consolidating power for a world <u>empire</u>. Let's examine several aspects of his coming.

A. He consolidates power through <u>military</u> might. There is no open hostility. His victories come through <u>diplomacy</u> (Rev. 6:1-2).

B. He comes promising world <u>peace</u> (1 Thess. 5:3).

C. He achieves power over a 10 nation <u>alliance</u> made up of countries represented by the Old Roman Empire (Dan. 2:42-44/ 7:23-26).

D. He comes with the blessing of <u>religion</u>, having established an unholy alliance with the apostate church. He later turns his attention to destroying religion (cf. Rev. 17).

E. One of his first official acts is an act of international peace. He signs a 7 year peace treaty with <u>Israel</u> promising to be her <u>protector</u> (Dan. 9:27).

F. He <u>breaks</u> this treaty after 3 1/2 years and becomes Israel's <u>persecutor</u> (Dan. 9:27).

G. Anti-Christian <u>ideologies</u> will prepare men's minds to receive the Devil's delusion (2 Thess. 3:12).

H. We are getting close to that time (2 Tim. 3:1-7).

Dr. J. Vernon McGee said, "The world will think it is entering the Millennium when it is really entering the Tribulation. The Great Tribulation will come in like a lamb, but go out like a lion" (p. 52). Even today with the Soviet Union dismantled, Japan economically strong, but militarily weak, Europe militarily strong, but dependent on the oil of the Middle East, the world is now ripe for the emergence of such a leader.

II. The Second Seal: World <u>War</u> 6:3-4

The second horseman rides a <u>red</u> horse. Red is often associated with <u>terror</u> and <u>death</u> (e.g.. red dragon 12:3, red beast 17:3). His purpose is to take peace from the earth. His agent is a "great sword" symbolizing <u>war</u>. Now comes open hostility (Rom. 3:17/ Matt. 24:6-7). The Anti-Christ's promise of peace is only a false peace and a temporary peace (Isa. 57:20-21).

III. The Third Seal: World <u>Hunger</u> 6:5-6

The third horseman rides a <u>black</u> horse symbolizing <u>famine</u> and <u>starvation</u>. The "scales" indicate a scarcity of food supplies, <u>rationing</u>, famine, hunger. A "quart of wheat for a denarius, and three quarts of barley for a denarius" In John's day a denarius was a day's wage. It would buy 8 quarts of wheat. There is apparently 1/8 of the normal food supply (<u>Revelation</u>, Ryrie, 45-46). Famine always follows war. Inflation tends to grip the economy after World War. There will be no food for the young or the elderly who can't work. People who have desired to live a life without God's help will get the chance. Anti-Christ will be able to control the economy since He will promise to feed the hungry masses. "Oil" refers to modern <u>toiletries</u>. "Wine" refers to <u>liquor</u>. These things enjoyed by the <u>wealthy</u> will be in abundance.

These next two seals reveal two very different destinies for people who die during the Tribulation.

IV. The Fourth Seal: World Wide <u>Death</u> 6:7-8

The fourth horseman rides a <u>pale</u> horse. He is the personification of Death and Hades. Death claims the <u>physical</u> part of man, the <u>body</u>, while Hades claims the <u>spiritual</u> part of man, the <u>soul</u>. Hades in Scripture is the place of punishment reserved for those who die apart from receiving Christ as Savior (Rev. 20:14). Christians need not fear Death or Hades since Jesus holds the keys (Rev. 1:18).

A. The <u>number</u> claimed by death   6:8   "a fourth"

In W W II one out of 40 people died.

During the Tribulation one out of 4 will die.

B. The <u>weapons</u> used by death   6:8

    1. the <u>sword</u>   v. 4

    2. <u>famine</u> v. 5-6

    3. <u>pestilence</u> v. 8

20 million died in the influenza epidemic of WWI

6 million died of typhus

Bacteria warfare is horrifying and available (Phillips, 103).

    4. wild beasts

This could be a reference to either the animal kingdom, or it could be referring to political leaders.

V. The Fifth Seal: World Wide <u>Persecution</u> 6:9-11

The fifth seal seems to be the world wide <u>persecution</u> and martyrdom of those who will choose to believe in God during the Tribulation period. The "altar" in verse 9 is in <u>heaven</u> (Rev. 14:18/ 16:7). People will be saved after the Rapture (cf. Rev. 7). Anti-Christ will instigate a mass persecution of Christians. Perhaps they will be seen as siding with an <u>alien</u> force. Perhaps it is because they refuse to receive the "<u>mark</u> of the beast." Perhaps it will be considered "<u>religious</u> cleansing."

    A. The <u>Reason</u> they were Martyred v.9

        1. "because of the Word of God" (cf. the apostle John, Rev. 1:9)

        2. "because of the testimony"

    B. The <u>Question</u> of the Martyred v.10-11

"How long...wilt Thou refrain from judging and avenging..."

The answer seems to be until evil has run its course. They are given a <u>white</u> <u>robe</u> and told that others will yet be martyred. Their question is the age old question of "Why evil?"

VI. The Sixth Seal: World Wide <u>Calamity</u> 6:12-17

Up until this point, the judgments are the results of <u>men</u> who are not restrained by God. The sixth seal is one that is definitely a <u>divine</u> judgment. It is characterized by great upheavals in the earth and the heavens.

    A. Upheavals in the <u>Earth</u> 6:12-14

        1. "a great earthquake" v.12

        This is the first of three earthquakes in Revelation (6:12/ 11:13/ 16:18-19).

        2. "every mountain and island were moved out of their places v.14

    B. Upheavals in the <u>Heavens</u> 6:12-14

        1. <u>Sun</u>= black as sackcloth

        2. <u>Moon</u>= like blood

        3. <u>Stars</u>= shaken from the sky

        4. <u>Sky</u>= split apart like a scroll

Notice all these similes using "like" and "as." This is *not* literal, but it is descriptive of what will actually be happening. When the sky is split apart like a scroll, some have suggested that men will see the heavens opened and catch a glimpse of God on His throne. Suddenly people will realize that they are being judged by God. It is the wrath of God and the wrath of   the Lamb (how paradoxical).

C. <u>Results</u> of this Judgment   6:15-17

This judgment is <u>worldwide</u> in its scope. It is not localized. It is universal. It affects all mankind. It even affects the rich and powerful (v.15).

    1. World Wide <u>Terror</u>   6:15-16

    2. Lack of <u>Repentance</u>   6:16

"hide us"

As awful as this is, Jesus says it is only the beginning of sorrows (Matt. 24:8).

The Tribulation will be a Day of <u>Wrath</u> (6:17).

Today is a Day of <u>Grace</u> (Eph. 2:8-9).

VII. The Seventh Seal

The Seventh Seal is not opened until chapter 8. It contains the seven <u>"trumpet"</u> judgments.

LESSON 9
GOD'S GRACE IN A DAY OF WRATH
(REVELATION 7:1-17)

The question is often asked, "Will people be saved during the Tribulation period?" Revelation chapter 7 answers this question. 2 Thessalonians 2:11,12 warns "And for this reason God will send upon them a deluding influence so that they might believe what is false, in order that they all may be judged who did not believe the truth, but took pleasure in wickedness." This passage leads many to believe that during the Tribulation period, those who have heard and rejected the gospel, will not be able to be saved. But the Scripture is clear that many will be saved during this period. Habakkuk 3:2 says, "In the midst of wrath, remember mercy." Though the Tribulation is a time of wrath, God's grace will still be available for some. In a way, Revelation chapter 7 is God's answer to the question in 6:17, "For the great day of their wrath has come; and who is able to stand?"

I. God is Gracious to the Jews   7:1-8

Grace means "unmerited favor." Salvation is a gift of God's grace (Eph. 2:8,9). Israel has been the apple of God's eye (Zech. 2:8). During the Tribulation period, He will be gracious to them. Many of the Jews will come to accept Jesus as their Messiah during those days. The Abrahamic Covenant is still in effect today (Gen. 12:1-3, Rom. 11:25-26, 29). Chapter 7 is a parenthesis in the judgments of the Tribulation. It appears to take place at the very beginning of the Tribulation. There will be 144,000 Jews who will be saved and sealed at that time.

   A. Gracious in Suspending Judgment   7:1

There is a lull in the impending storm of God's wrath. "Angels" in Revelation often are dispensing wrath or holding it back. God suspends His judgment for the purpose of showing His grace.

   B. Gracious in Sealing the Jews   7:2-7

God loves the Jews. He still has a future for them.

(He also loves you and has a future for you.)

      1. What is a Seal?

It is a <u>mark</u> or a <u>brand</u>.

Where? on the <u>Forehead</u>

Visible or Invisible?   I don't know. "A seal does not have to be visible to be real" (<u>Revelation</u>, Ryrie, 50), (Eph. 1:13-14/ 4:30).

This seal stands in contrast to the <u>Mark</u> of the Beast.

The Devil has his mark and God has His (2 Tim. 2:19).

2. Who is Sealed?

144,000 <u>Jews</u>. John is very specific about these numbers and in identifying these people. There are 12,000 from 12 different tribes. These are *literal* numbers and *literal* Jews. There is no reason in the passage to take it otherwise. This is right in line with the Old Testament promises to Israel. This is *not* the church.

3. Why are they sealed?

A seal in that day was placed on a document or a piece of property as a mark of <u>ownership</u> and <u>protection</u>.

    a. To <u>shield</u>   A supernatural protection from <u>Anti-Christ</u>.

    b. To <u>secure</u>   They will "call upon the name of the Lord and be saved" (Rom. 10:13), perhaps like Paul on the Damascus Road (1 Cor. 15:8). Their <u>salvation</u> is secure.

    c. To <u>select</u>   This is a mark of <u>identification</u>, much like baptism today is a public mark of identification with Christ and His church. They are selected to be spared from the wrath of God and the Anti-Christ.

    d. To <u>serve</u>   They are called "bondservants." This same word was used by Paul and by James to describe themselves. Bondservants of Christ have a <u>message</u> to spread, the Gospel (1 Cor. 4:1). If you're saved, you are also a bondservant. You have been saved to serve. Are you spreading the gospel (cf. Matt. 24:14)?

II. God is Gracious to the <u>Gentiles</u> 7:9-17

God loves the Jews and has a plan for them (Rom. 11:2, 12, 29). Paul considered himself as a Jew who was born prematurely (1 Cor. 15:8). He may have been referring to the future time when Israel would turn to Jesus as their Messiah and Savior (Rom. 11:25,26). Just imagine 144,000 "Pauls" evangelizing the world. "The greatest Revival the world has ever known is yet to come" (LaHaye 109). This passage describes a vast number of Gentiles who will turn to Jesus during the Tribulation period. Many of them will pay with their lives.

    A. A People of Every <u>Race</u> 7:9, 13-14

        1. Their <u>number</u>   "a great number which no one could count."

        2. Their <u>mixture</u>   "from every nation and all tribes and peoples and tongues"

    There are no <u>racial</u> barriers to the doors of heaven.

    Some of us may have to make some adjustments.

        3. Their <u>identity</u>   "These are the ones who come out of the great tribulation" v.14

4. Their <u>purchase price</u> "the blood of the Lamb" v. 14

B. A <u>Place</u> of Absolute Grace   7:9b

    1. They are "standing before the throne and before the Lamb."

    2. They are clothed in "white robes," symbolizing <u>righteousness</u>. (Rev.3:4,5,18/ 6:11/ 7:14) These are not the filthy rags of <u>self</u>-righteousness, but the white robes of Christ's righteousness (Phil. 3:9). That is grace. There will be no boasting in Heaven (Eph. 2:8-9).

    3. They have "palm branches" in their hands. This speaks of victory, rejoicing, and <u>worship</u>. (e.g.. the Triumphal Entry)

C. A <u>Praise</u> Chorus of His Grace   7:10-12

These redeemed saints from the "great tribulation" are singing a chorus of praise to their Savior.

    1. The chorus of the <u>redeemed</u>   v. 10

    2. The chorus of the <u>angels</u> v. 12

The angels do not experience <u>salvation</u> since they are *not* fallen creatures. They do rejoice in our salvation, and the victory wrought by God over Satan.

They are singing "Victory in Jesus."

Those who receive the Mark of the Beast will be singing "Almost Persuaded."

D. A <u>Provision</u> from His Grace   7:15-17

Have you ever wondered what Heaven will be like for the Christian? John gives us a little insight into it here as we look at these Tribulation saints.

    1. They are <u>serving</u>   v.15a

Heaven is a place of <u>activity</u>, not inactivity.

    2. They are <u>satisfied</u>   v.15b,16

Jesus spreads His tabernacle of protection over them. They are not subject to the <u>trials</u> they experienced on earth.

    3. They are <u>soothed</u>   v. 17

"God shall wipe every tear from their eyes."

In Heaven we will be soothed by our "shepherd." Ironically, the "Lamb" will be our "shepherd" (cf. Ps. 23). We will be soothed by God personally wiping our tears and removing our suffering and sorrow. We will be soothed by the cool, refreshing, life sustaining "water of life." How precious to those who have suffered from extreme thirst like those Tribulation saints. Those first century saints who originally received this letter and were also experiencing persecution must have been greatly encouraged by this message of hope for the future.

Conclusion:

Many will be saved during the Tribulation, Jews and Gentiles. The great multitude who are saved will have to experience martyrdom. It is hard to understand why some will *not* believe when faced with these great judgments. But it is hard to understand why people refuse to receive His free gift of salvation today. What makes the difference between these people. It is the difference between wax and clay. They same sun that softens wax, hardens clay. These people will all face the same trials, yet some will repent and others will rebel. Are you wax or clay? *Does God's Word soften you or harden you? Why not come to Him today?*

LESSON
10 TRUMPETS OF JUDGMENT (PART 1)
(REVELATION 8:1-13)

Chapter 7 was a parenthesis in John's development of the Tribulation. Chapters 8 and 9 continue the chronological movement through the Tribulation which was begun in chapter 6 with a discussion of the seven seals. Chapters 8 and 9 discuss the seven trumpet judgments. These seven trumpet judgments are not the same as the seven seal judgments. The trumpets pick up where the seals left off. They also seem to increase in severity. They are divine judgments, not just man-made catastrophes like some of the seal judgments.

I. The Seventh <u>Seal</u>   8:1-6

A. The <u>Sequence</u>

The seven sealed book is now fully <u>opened</u>. The sequence of judgment is the 7 <u>seals</u> in chapter 6 followed by the 7 <u>trumpets</u> in chapters 8 and 9 followed by 7 <u>bowls</u> in chapter 16. It appears that the seventh seal <u>contains</u> the 7 trumpets and the seventh trumpet <u>contains</u> the 7 bowls.

B. The <u>Silence</u>   8:1

Someone has said this verse proves that there will be no <u>women</u> in heaven since they could not keep quiet this long (ha). Silence is not the usual sound of Heaven. It is usually <u>rejoicing</u>. This is the silence of "expectancy" and "foreboding" (<u>Revelation</u>, Ryrie, 55). It indicates the importance of this event. This is the still before the storm.

C. The <u>Seven Angels</u>   8:2

These seven attending angels before the throne of God are in readiness for the Lord's command. During this time of silence they receive trumpets announcing judgment. In the Promised Land, Israel used trumpets for two primary purposes. One was a call to <u>war</u>, and the other was a call to <u>worship</u> (Numbers 10:9-10). The trumpet used to announce the Rapture (2 Thess. 4:17) is a call to <u>worship</u> for the Christian. The trumpets used in chapters 8 and 9 are a call to <u>war</u> on rebellious unbelievers.

D. The <u>Smoke</u>   8:3-4

The smoke of the <u>prayers</u> of believers ascends before the throne of God. The "censor" is made of gold, like the one in Solomon's Temple. It was the custom to use the "censor" to bring hot coals from the brazen altar outside to the altar of incense on the inside. Then incense was carried to the altar and poured over the hot coals which produced a fragrant smoke. This incense referred to here is the "<u>prayers</u> of all the <u>saints</u>" (cf. 6:10). The "saints" are *not* an elite group, rather they are <u>all</u> Christians. (There are only 2 kinds of people, the "saints", and the "ain'ts." Which kind are you?) What was their prayer? Perhaps it was "Thy Kingdom come, Thy will be done on earth" (Matt. 6:10).

E. The <u>Storm</u> 8:5-6

The prayer <u>ascended</u>, and the judgment <u>descended</u>. The angel threw the fire from the altar to the earth. Fire is sometimes a symbol of <u>judgment</u>. "Thunder" and "lightning" are warnings of a coming <u>storm</u>. There is a gathering storm cloud of judgment as the 7 angels prepare to sound the seven trumpets.

II. The First Trumpet 8:7 (The Earth)

Someone has suggested that these judgments are symbolic. However, symbols in Scripture are usually stated. These results seem real. What about the Plagues of Egypt? They were not symbolic, and neither were their results.

A. The <u>Judgment</u>

This plague contains hail and fire mixed with blood. It affects the land surface and brings devastation to the earth.

B. The <u>Results</u>

1/3 of the <u>earth</u> burned

1/3 of <u>trees</u> burned

all the green <u>grass</u> burned

This is an ecological disaster as well as an economic disaster since it would destroy the farming industry. Modern warfare deliberately destroys plant life now to destroy the enemy's cover (Phillips, 119). The first world wide judgment came by a <u>flood</u>, this one comes by a <u>fire</u> (2 Pet. 3:6-7).

III. The Second Trumpet 8:8-9 (The Sea)

A. The <u>Judgment</u>

"Something <u>like</u> a great mountain" was thrown into the sea. What is this? John does not say it is a mountain, he just uses a mountain to describe it. It could be some powerful bomb. It is more likely a <u>heavenly</u> projectile. It is something that the earth has not experienced before. This judgment is aimed at the <u>sea</u>.

B. The <u>Results</u>

1/3 of the <u>sea</u> became blood

1/3 of the <u>creatures</u> in the sea died

1/3 of the <u>ships</u> were destroyed

People who interpret this symbolically have a hard time with the <u>ships</u>. In January 1 1981, there were 24,867 ocean going merchant ships. One third would be 8, 289 ships suddenly destroyed with their cargoes of animals, people, weapons, food, and oil (Wiersbe, 593).

IV. The Third Trumpet 8:10-11   (The Fresh Water)

A. The <u>Judgment</u>

A great <u>star</u> fell from Heaven. Some have taken this <u>symbolically</u> to refer to Satan himself. I tend to take it <u>literally </u>since the results are described literally. This appears to be some meteor burning its way through our atmosphere, exploding, falling and spreading its fatal fallout to the side of the planet that it hits.

B. The <u>Results</u>

1/3 of the fresh <u>water</u> is polluted

many men died from the waters

The star is called Wormwood after a kind of wood mentioned in the Old Testament that caused water to taste bitter. In the Old Testament bitterness is associated with <u>sorrow</u> and <u>judgment</u> (cf. Ruth 1:20-21). This star does more than make the water taste <u>bitter</u>, it also makes it <u>poison</u>.

V. The Fourth Trumpet 8:12-13   (The Skies and the Heavens)

A. The <u>Judgment</u>

1/3 of the <u>sun</u>

1/3 of the <u>moon</u>

1/3 of the <u>stars</u>

B. The <u>Result</u>

1/3 of the <u>daylight</u> is removed.

Whether this means that the <u>wattage</u> is turned down by one third, or whether the sun shines for one third <u>less</u> of the day, I don't know. Either way, it is a very emphatic way for God to get mankind's attention (Amos 5:18/ Joel 2:1-2). The result will be dark days and black nights.

Since mankind has rejected the light of Jesus Christ and prefers <u>moral</u> and <u>spiritual</u> darkness, God sends them <u>physical</u> darkness as well.

John 3:19 "Men loved darkness rather than light, for their deeds were evil."

Matthew 24:29 "But immediately after the tribulation of those days, the sun will be darkened, and the moon will not give its light, and the stars will fall from the sky, and the powers of the heavens will be shaken."   (Jesus)

VI. Announcement of <u>Woe</u>   8:13

This Eagle can speak. Apparently its speech is understood by the inhabitants of the earth. Perhaps it is the Eagle like creature mentioned in 4:7-8 (Wiersbe, 594). He has a message of "woe." "Woe" is a warning of <u>judgment</u> to come (e.g.. Matt. 11:24/ Mark 14:21/ Rev. 18: 10, 16, 19). This threefold woe speaks of the <u>certainty</u> of the judgment yet to come. It is going to be more severe than that which has already taken place. "The worst is yet to come." These three "woes" refer to the last three <u>trumpet</u> judgments (cf. 9:12). The last three angels who sound their trumpets will announce "woes."

"Those who dwell on the earth" is a technical phrase John uses that is found 12 times in Revelation (Wiersbe, 594). It does not merely refer to where these people live. It refers to a certain <u>kind</u> of person. They are <u>earthly</u> people, *not* <u>heavenly</u> people. They are people who care only for earthly things, and not for the things of Heaven.

What kind of person are you? Are you earthly-minded, or heavenly-minded? Where is your focus?

LESSON 11
TRUMPETS OF JUDGMENT (PART 2)
(REVELATION 9:1-21/ 11:15-19)

The Trumpet judgments found in Revelation chapters 8 and 9 represent the second wave of judgments during the Tribulation period. The first wave was the 7 seals found in chapter 6. Last week we discussed the first four Trumpets and their consequences for mankind. This week we will discuss the last three Trumpets which are also called the three "Woes."

I. The Fifth Trumpet 9:1-12 The First <u>Woe</u>......<u>Abuse</u> from the Abyss

Man's <u>rebellion</u> against God gets progressively <u>worse</u> and so do these judgments.   Some have asked if people will get a second chance after death. Why should they? Their answer would be the <u>same</u> (LaHaye,133). Someone has described this period as "Hell let loose on earth."

    A. The <u>Loosing</u> of the Creatures   9:1-3

"star" This can refer to a heavenly <u>body</u> or a <u>person</u> (e.g. Clint Eastwood is a star.).

"him" This star is a <u>person</u>.

"fallen" (cf. Isa. 14:12-15/ Luke 10:18)

"was given to him" His power is given to him, thus it is <u>limited</u>. Who gives him this power? The One who holds the keys to death and hades (1:18), and who will eventually consign Satan himself to the pit (20:3).

"bottomless pit"   Literally, "the shaft of the abyss" This refers to a very <u>real</u> place. It is mentioned 7 times in Revelation. It is also mentioned in Luke 8:31 and Romans 10:7.

"like" "as"   These two words showing comparison are used more in this chapter than any other chapter in the Bible. It shows just how difficult it was for John to describe what he saw here (McGee, 73).

"locusts"   They have the power of scorpions to sting and inflict pain. Some have tried to <u>modernize</u> this to refer to aircraft. It seems to refer to <u>demonic</u> creatures who are designed to inflict pain upon humanity.   There are two types of <u>demons</u> referred to in the Bible, those who are at work in the world, and those who are confined in "chains of darkness" (2 Pet. 2:4) (LaHaye, 135).

Will they be <u>visible</u>? They were seen by John who was in the Spirit. Elisha saw an army of angels (2 Kings 6:17). They are spirit beings and may or may not be visible to men.

B. The Limitation of the Creatures   9:4-6

Humanly speaking there is no defense against these devilish creatures. They are incapable of being killed. They are too intelligent to hide from. They are too swift to run from. Because of their hatred for humanity, they show no mercy. But their activity will be limited by God.

1. They cannot harm <u>nature</u>.   9:4

2. They cannot hurt <u>men</u> who have the <u>seal</u> of God.   9:4

3. They cannot <u>kill</u> anyone.   9:5

4. They cannot <u>stay</u> more than <u>five</u> months.   9:5

C. The <u>Likeness</u> of the Creatures   9:7-10

Some have tried to <u>modernize</u> this description to mean hippies on Harleys. Others have tried to <u>spiritualize</u> it away as referring to the effects of living life without Christ. But these are demonic creatures, possibly unseen by human eyes. They are ferocious, yet they are still subject to God's control.

D. The <u>Leader</u> of the Creatures   9:11

These demons have a leader and his name is "Abaddon," or "Apollyon" which means "<u>destruction</u>." Some have suggested that it refers to Satan, but since he arises out of the Abyss, and we know that Satan is not there yet, then it may refer to one of Satan's evil generals (cf. John 10:10).

II. The Sixth Trumpet   9:13-19   The Second <u>Woe</u> - <u>Death</u> from the Demons

The sixth Trumpet signals a second invading army. This army comes to kill and destroy.

A. The Angels' <u>Release</u>   9:13-15

1. The <u>Command</u> from God   9:13-14

There are 4 evil angels which have been bound by God. Good angels would not have been bound (2 Pet. 2:4/ Jude 6). The perfect tense of the verb indicates that they <u>were</u> bound and <u>continue</u> to <u>remain</u> bound. Why were they not released earlier? They were reserved for the day of judgment (Jude 6). Why didn't Satan release them? He is <u>unable</u>. They have an intense <u>hatred</u> for humanity, perhaps because mankind is the special object of God's love (John 3:16). They have great power and influence and marshal a huge army.

2. The <u>Consequences</u> for Mankind   9:15

1/3 of mankind <u>slain</u>

The Fourth seal proclaimed 1/4 of the population slain. These two judgments combined account for 1/2 of the population. Those slain are no doubt the <u>incorrigibles</u> who would never trust Christ and would serve only as a <u>hindrance</u> to the undecided.

B. The Army's <u>Ruthlessness</u>   9:16-19

1. Their <u>number</u>

200 Million Man March

They are led by 4 Evil Angels. This could be a <u>human</u> army. Red China boasts an army of 200 million. It could be a <u>demonic</u> army. Or it could be men driven by demons.

2. Their <u>nature</u>

These horses and riders seem supernatural, *not* natural. Some have tried to <u>modernize</u> this interpretation by saying John really saw guns and missiles which were totally unknown in John's day.

Assuming the population after the Rapture is 5 Billion. Then 1.25 Billion would die in the fourth seal, and another 1.25 Billion would die during the sixth Trumpet. This is one half of the world's population in these two judgments.

III. The <u>Stubbornness</u> of the Survivors 9:20-21

One would expect after this display of divine judgment, and seeing Satan's outright hatred for mankind, that men and women would <u>repent</u>. They "did *not* repent" (v. 21). They refused to repent of two specific things:

A. Their <u>Idolatry</u> 9:20

They worshipped demons and idols.

B. Their <u>Iniquity</u> 9:21

"murder" Christianity places a high value on <u>human</u> life.

"sorceries" This refers to <u>occult</u> practices. The word literally refers to drug and alcohol use which is often associated with the occult.

"immorality" This refers to <u>sexual</u> promiscuity. This is today's philosophy of life.

"thefts" This refers to <u>stealing</u> as a way of life.   It will be a crime ridden culture.

IV. The Seventh Trumpet 11:15-19

The Seventh Trumpet is an announcement that the end is near. It appears that the seven bowl judgments of chapters 15 and 16 proceed from the Seventh Trumpet Judgment.

It is important to remember that these last two judgments are <u>Satanic</u> judgments. This is what Satan would like to do now if he could. Only the gracious hand of a loving God is restraining and limiting these forces of evil.

LESSON 12
THE LITTLE BOOK (WITH THE BIG MESSAGE)
(REVELATION 10:1-11)

In Revelation chapter 10, John receives and consumes a little book that is given to him by an angel. It is reminiscent of a similar incident in the life of Ezekiel and Jeremiah. This little book has a big message that is both bitter and sweet. It is the word of God and that is sometimes pleasant and sometimes difficult. We will see how it affects John, and how it may affect us.

I. The Courier of the Book   10:1-6

This courier is a strong angel coming down out of heaven.

A. His Appearance   10:1

His livery is that of royalty. Some have claimed that this is Christ Himself (cf. chapter 1). He is described as a "strong angel." In the O. T. Christ is seen in angelic form, but never after His incarnation. John does not bow down to this angel as He does to Christ in chapter 1. This "strong angel" must be the special envoy of Christ to earth, bringing a special message, and wearing the credentials of Heaven (McGee 80).

B. His Action   10:2-3

He is bringing a little book. Perhaps it is the same book as in chapter 5. Perhaps it contains further revelation. It is an open book. It is the angel's authority for what he does. He places one foot on the sea, and another on the land, symbolically claiming the planet for Christ. This earth belongs to the Lord (Psalm 24:1-2).

Application: Do you own some property down here? Don't get carried away with it. It doesn't really belong to you.

C. His Accompaniment   10:3-4

He is accompanied by seven peals of thunder. Thunder is usually the harbinger of a coming storm. These are obviously heavenly voices that thunder out a message. Their message, however, is sealed. This is the only thing in the book of Revelation that is   sealed.

D. His Affirmation   10:5-6

He lifted his right hand. He is a <u>witness</u> about to give a <u>testimony</u>. He is giving a sworn statement. He swears by Jesus Christ (cf. John 1:1-3). This gives another indication that the angel is *not* Jesus(cf. Heb. 6:13).

This earth belongs to Christ by right of <u>creation</u>. He made it and it belongs to Him. It has been usurped by <u>Satan</u>, but Christ intends to reclaim it. He made it from nothing. "There shall be delay no longer." "Time, "or "delay," here means a period of time(cf. Matt. 24:2). Remember the question of 6:2, "How long?" The angel is stating that Jesus is getting ready to wrap it up. Why is He delaying today? So people can be saved (cf. 2 Peter 3:1-9, 15).

II. The <u>Contents</u> of the Little Book   10:7-11

A. The <u>Idea</u> of the Book   10:7

The idea of the book is that the "Mystery of God is finished." In the Scripture, a "mystery" is a <u>previously</u> <u>hidden</u> <u>truth</u> that has now been <u>revealed</u>. This "mystery" has been preached to his servants the prophets." It refers to the coming Kingdom and the final fulfillment of all the promises of God. It refers to the "How," and the "specifics" of it. Some have suggested that the mystery is "Why was Evil tolerated?" (cf. 6:10).

B. The <u>Instruction</u> of the Book   10:8-10

The book must be <u>digested</u>. It must be personally <u>received</u>. For other similar cases see Jer. 15:16/ Ezek. 2:8-3:4/ Ps. 119:103. Notice that John says it is "<u>sweet</u>." The word of God is sweet to study. It is "sweet" to learn a new truth from God. It is "sweet" to know that God is <u>real</u>. It is "sweet" to know that <u>salvation</u> is sure. He also says it is "<u>bitter</u>." It is "bitter" to know that <u>judgment</u> is coming, and people are going to get hurt. It is "bitter" to know that <u>Hell</u> is real. *No* preacher with the mind of Christ and the compassion of Christ enjoys bringing a message of judgment. It is a bitter pill.

C. The <u>Imperative</u> of the Book   10:11

"You *must* prophesy again." By now John is tired of bringing a message of severe judgment, but there is still more to come, and it is worse. It is a prophecy concerning "many peoples and nations and tongues and kings." God's Word affects <u>everybody</u>. God's Word applies to <u>everybody</u>. No one is exempt.

Conclusion:

1. Before the preacher or teacher can minister the word of God, he must personally experience it, just like John did.

2. Just like the little book was sweet in John's mouth and bitter in his stomach, God's word is often pleasant, but it often bring s a message of heaviness. Not every truth in God's word is designed to make you happy. It is designed to make you more Christlike (Rom. 8:29).

3. The return of Christ is one of the most exciting doctrines in the Bible. It is also one of the most frightening. I'm excited about going to be with Christ someday. I'm also worried about what will happen to others who are not ready when He comes.

4. Right now Christ is delaying His coming. Why is He waiting? So you will have time to turn to Him in faith and be saved. And so Christians will have time to get the gospel out to a lost world

(2 Pet. 3:1-9, 15). Take advantage of this delay, by trusting Christ *now* and sharing Christ with others who are lost.

LESSON 13
THE TRIBULATION TEMPLE
(REVELATION 11:1-2)

The Great Tribulation is called the "time of Jacob's sorrow," and Daniel's seventieth week. This is because much of what goes on is designed to bring Israel back to God. Even now many Jews are turning to Jesus. Many others are beginning to search for spiritual truth. Chapter 11 deals with the spiritual life of Israel during the Tribulation by discussing the testimony of the Temple, and the testimony of the two witnesses. Chapter 12 will deal with the coming persecution of Israel.

I. The <u>History</u> of the Temple

Revelation 11:1-2 seems to indicate that the Temple will be rebuilt in Jerusalem and that Old Testament worship will be re-instituted. Let's take a look at the history of the Temple in the Old Testament.

A. <u>David</u> desired to build a Temple for God (2 Sam. 7:1-17).

B. <u>Solomon</u> did build a Temple using the plans and much of the material that David had gathered (1 Kings 6-7). "The nation thought itself impregnable as long as the Temple stood." (LaHaye, <u>Revelation</u> Illustrated and Made Plain, 148).

C. The Temple was destroyed by the <u>Babylonians</u> during their third invasion of the city in 586 BC (2 Kings 25:11-21).

D. Seventy years later under the <u>Persians</u> there was a decree to rebuild the Temple (Ezra 1:1-3). It was rebuilt in the days of <u>Zerubbabel</u> the governor, and <u>Joshua</u> the priest (Ezra 3-6). It was much <u>inferior</u> to Solomon's Temple and the older men who could remember Solomon's Temple cried when they saw it (Ezra 3:12-13). (LaHaye, 149).

E. This Temple served Israel while they were under the <u>Persians</u> and also under the <u>Greeks</u>. The Greek ruler, Antiochus Epiphanes, desecrated this temple by sacrificing a <u>sow</u> on the altar and setting up a statue of <u>Zeus</u> in the Holy of Holies. This was the "abomination of desolation" that Daniel described in Daniel 11:31. Jesus warned that the <u>Anti-Christ</u> would desecrate the Temple in a similar way (Matt. 24:15).

Under the leadership of the Jewish Maccabeas, the Temple was recaptured and cleansed. The Jews celebrate this recovery of the Temple each year in the holiday, <u>Hanukkah</u>.

F. <u>Herod</u> the Great had this temple destroyed piecemeal and rebuilt. It was magnificent. Herod was a great builder. It was still under construction during the days of <u>Jesus</u>. It was called Herod's Temple (LaHaye, 149).

G. Jesus predicted that Herod's Temple would be <u>destroyed</u> (Matt. 24:2).

H. This Temple was destroyed true to Jesus' prophecy by the Roman General Titus in <u>70</u> AD within 40 years of Jesus' crucifixion.

II. <u>Predictions</u> Concerning the Temple

These passages indicate that the Temple *will* be standing during the Tribulation period. While they do *not* prophesy its rebuilding, they <u>assume</u> that it will be in existence during that time.

A. Daniel 9:24-27   This passage refers to the <u>Tribulation</u> period and the activities of <u>Anti-Christ</u>. It indicates that he will put an end to their <u>public</u> <u>sacrifice</u> and desolate the Temple like Antiochus Epiphanes also did.

B. Matthew 24:15   Here Jesus refers to Daniel 9:27 and says that it is still <u>future</u>. He actually says that the <u>Anti-Christ</u> will be "standing in the holy place."

C. 2 Thessalonians 2:2-4   This passage claims that the <u>Anti-Christ</u> will "take his seat in the temple of God" and there will proclaim himself to be a <u>god</u>.

D. Revelation 11:1-2   In this passage which takes place during the <u>Tribulation</u>, John is asked to <u>measure</u> the Temple.

Apparently this Temple will be rebuilt and <u>Old</u> <u>Testament</u> worship re-instituted in it either <u>before</u> the Tribulation *or* <u>early</u> in the Tribulation.

III. The <u>Construction</u> of the Temple

A. This Temple will be constructed by the Jews in <u>unbelief</u>.

B. Christians do not need a Temple in which to worship.

According to 1 Corinthians 6:19-20, the individual <u>Christian</u> *is* God's temple which is indwelt by the Holy Spirit. The church as a corporate body of believers is also referred to as God's Temple (1 Pet. 2:5). Our church building is a place to meet, and a place set aside for the purpose of worshipping God, but it is *not* a Temple.

C. It is possible that the Temple will be built <u>before</u> the Rapture of the Church.

That would be exciting since it would be a further evidence that God's word will be fulfilled. It is also possible that the Temple could be built at the <u>beginning</u> of the Tribulation. Scripture says that the Anti-Christ will sign a <u>seven</u> year peace treaty with Israel at the beginning of the Tribulation period (Dan. 9:27). He will pledge to <u>protect</u> them from their aggressive neighbors. Part of this treaty *could* include the building of their Temple on Temple Mount in Jerusalem. Trying to rebuild it now could cause a war since two Moslem shrines now occupy the Temple Mount. The Dome of the Rock and the Mosque of Omar currently occupy the space.

D. <u>Measuring</u> of the Temple   11:1

1. Measuring shows a <u>claim</u> (Wiersbe 598).

You measure something you are going to claim, like property.

2. Measuring shows <u>inadequacy</u> (LaHaye, 150) (cf. Dan. 5:27).

The *Temple* doesn't measure up to the finished work of <u>Christ</u> Heb. 10:1-4,10). The *Altar* doesn't measure up to the <u>Cross</u> (Heb. 9:8-14). The *worshippers* don't measure up since their worship is based on <u>works</u> and *not* <u>faith</u>. Without faith it is impossible to please God (Heb. 11:6).

3. The <u>outer</u> <u>court</u> is left unmeasured.   11:2

This was the <u>Gentile</u> court. The prediction is made that the Gentiles will tread the Temple under foot for 42 months, or three and one-half years. This corresponds to the last half of the <u>Tribulation</u> period, after the Anti-Christ has broken his <u>seven</u> year treaty. Jesus predicted that Jerusalem would be trodden under foot by the Gentiles (Luke 21:24). The "times of the Gentiles" <u>began</u> in 606 BC when the Babylonians conquered Judah and will continue till Jesus returns at the <u>end</u> of the Tribulation.

The following is taken from <u>One World Under Anti-Christ</u> by Peter Lalonde p. 263.

Today the call for just such a rebuilding is making the headlines. The riot on the Temple mount in late 1990 ignited when Arabs claimed to have believed a rumor that a group called "The Temple Mount Faithful" were going to lay a cornerstone for the rebuilding of Solomon's Temple. The following articles from the Associated Press and the Jerusalem Post are indicative of how the groundwork for such a rebuilding is being laid. According to the Associated Press article:

Hoping to rebuild the ancient Jewish Temple where Islamic shrines now stand, a group of Israeli rabbis are compiling computerized lists of potential priests, weaving seamless linen robes and reproducing a gemstudded breastplate described in Exodus.

"All Jewish history as far as we're concerned is one big parenthesis until the temple is returned," said Rabbi Nahman Kahane of the Temple Institute. ...

The Temple Institute's 50 rabbis and artisans have made Temple vessels and produced a computerized blueprint of the shrine in preparation for rebuilding it on the site where it stood until A. D. 70, when the Romans destroyed it.

More than $200,000 has been collected to finance the project, most of it from American Jews, according to institute director Rabbi Yisrael Ariel.

The Post article updates these efforts:

Led by a cohen in priestly robes, and equipped with special vessels for the Temple ritual, two ram's horns, a clarinet and an accordion, members of the Faithful of the Temple Mount marched last week from the Western Wall to the

Pool of Siloam to consecrate what they have designated as the cornerstone of the Third Temple.

Police had prevented the group from laying the "cornerstone" in the Western Wall Plaza, as they originally intended.

The one-metre-cube stone, which in accordance with the biblical precept was not hewn with an iron tool, was donated by Zion and Ezra Alafi, stone-cutters on Jerusalem's Hanevi'im Street. ...During the procession, the three-ton stone lay on a flatbed truck which followed the group down the steep narrow road through Silwan village, past walls covered with graffiti in support of the intifada. Only a few local residents came out of their homes to watch scores of flag-waving marchers, almost outnumbered by police, newsmen and photographers.

At the spring, Yehoshua Cohen, a member of the priestly cast, wearing the woven linen priestly robes, drew water, as Gershon Salomon, leader of the FTM, led the group in reciting the sheheheyanu blessing, in which one gives thanks for having reached a special occasion. The robes and vessels were prepared by Yeshivat Habayit, which is dedicated to studying the practical aspects of restoring the Temple.

Another group, the Movement to Establish the Sanctuary, was represented by Yisrael Schneider, a Bratislav hassid, wearing the striped robes of the old Jerusalem Ashkenazi community.

Get Ready 'Cause Jesus is Coming Back Soon!

LESSON 14
THE TWO WITNESSES
(REVELATION 11:3-14)

The ministry of the two witnesses mentioned in Revelation chapter 11 is a question that has intrigued many Bible students over the centuries. Many are curious as to their identity, but also to the time of their ministry. We will examine these things and the importance of their ministry during the Tribulation.

I. Their <u>Divine</u> <u>Authority</u>   11:3-6

    A. Their <u>Authority</u> is from God.   11:3-4

"witnesses"   Their ministry is particularly to <u>Israel</u> and <u>Jerusalem</u>.

"two"   This was the required number of witnesses (Deut.17:6/Matt.18:16).

"Prophesy"   They will forecast the <u>future</u>. They will also speak against the moral and spiritual <u>evil</u> of their day.

"1260 days"   This corresponds to 42 months, or <u>3 and 1/2</u> years (lunar years). The duration of their ministry is clear. Whether they minister during the first or second half of the Tribulation is *not* clear. Ryrie and McGee believe it is the first half, Walvoord believes the second half, Pentecost does not commit.

"clothed in sackcloth"   This indicates <u>mourning</u> for their nation, and repentance.

"two olive trees"   They are <u>anointed</u> of God.

"two lampstands"   They are <u>shining</u> for God. These two figures of speech are also used of Zerubbabel the governor, and Joshua the priest who rebuilt the Temple after the Babylonian exile (Zech 4:3,11,14).

    B. Their <u>Activity</u> is for God.   11:5-6

        1. They have <u>divine</u> <u>protection</u>.

        This is reminiscent of Elijah in 2 Kings 1:9-14.

        2. They have <u>divine</u> <u>powers</u>.

These are like those manifested by the Old Testament prophets such as Elijah and Moses, both of whom faced tyrannical leaders.

3. What is their _identity_?

Four Suggestions:

(1) <u>Elijah</u> and <u>Moses</u>:   Mal. 4:5 predicts that Elijah will come. Matt. 17:10-13 Jesus says that Elijah will come. He also says that John the Baptist fulfilled this prophecy (Matt. 11:14). These witnesses have a similar ministry to that of Moses and Elijah. Moses and Elijah met with Christ on the Mount of Transfiguration. The body of Moses was never discovered (Jude 9).

(2) <u>Elijah</u> and <u>Enoch</u>:   These two men both escaped death (Heb. 9:27). Both of these men preached in days of great godlessness (Jude 14).

(3) <u>Elijah</u> and <u>John</u> the <u>Baptist</u>:   McGee suggests John the Baptist since he was Christ's forerunner at His first coming. Both stood against impossible odds, and stood alone for God. (McGee, 88)

(4) <u>Two</u> <u>new</u> <u>men</u>:   It is none of these men. Rather, they are two individuals who are not yet on the scene. Just as John the Baptist came in the spirit and power of Elijah and fulfilled the prophecy of Malachi 4:5, God will raise up two more prophets in the spirit and power of Elijah to resist the Anti-Christ.

Summary: That they are two <u>human</u> witnesses with <u>mortal</u> bodies is clear from this passage. That they will have <u>supernatural</u> powers from God to battle the Anti-Christ and to speak out for God is also true. That they will have <u>ministries</u> similar to those of Elijah and Moses is clear. Their identity is _not_ evident from this passage and is _not_ necessary to a correct understanding of the book of Revelation.

II. Their <u>Devilish</u> <u>Enemy</u> 11:7-10

   A. Their <u>Enemy</u>   "the beast out of the abyss" 11:7

   This is a reference to the <u>Anti-Christ</u>.

   At the <u>midpoint</u> of the Tribulation period Anti-Christ invades Israel, persecutes Israel, kills the two witnesses, and desecrates the <u>Temple</u>. (This supposes that their ministry is during the first half of the Tribulation.) God allows this. They "finished their testimony." A witness gives his <u>testimony</u>. These men testify concerning Christ. Only when their work is <u>finished</u> does God allow them to be <u>martyred</u>. The man of God is indestructible till His work is finished.

   B. Their <u>Martyrdom</u> 11:8-10

      1. Where: <u>Jerusalem</u>

      "Sodom"=wickedness   "Egypt"=worldliness and materialism

      2. How: Their bodies will be left in the <u>street</u>.

      Their bodies will be for public viewing like some sick trophy.

      3. How long: <u>3,1/2</u> days

The whole world will see them? The technology of TV could make this possible.

4. Why: A Satanic Celebration

"Those who dwell on the earth" refers to the Christ rejecters. They are rejoicing. This will be interpreted as a victory by the Anti-Christ over God.

III. Their Destined Victory 11:11-13

God is going to crash their party. He is going to turn it into an evangelistic event.

A. A Resurrection 11:11

As the unbelieving crowd looks on, these two witnesses are resurrected and stand up. "Great fear" comes upon that crowd.

B. A Rapture 11:12

Everyone hears a supernatural "voice from heaven" which says to the two witnesses "come up here." These are the same words that John heard in Revelation 4:1. These witnesses will be raptured into "the cloud" (the Shekinah glory of God as in the Old Testament and as in the ascension of Christ, cf. Acts 1).

C. A Revival 11:13

This event is followed by a devastating earthquake which destroys one tenth of Jerusalem. This earthquake kills 7,000 Jerusalemites. "The rest" seem to have a conversion experience. This may be the event that causes Israel to turn to Jesus as their Messiah (Romans 11:26).

Even in the worst of times God will have His witness. And His witness will be heard. It is much better to turn to God today in a day of grace, than to wait for this severe witness that must come. Perhaps the Anti-Christ is alive today preparing for his ominous rise to power.

LESSON 15
PUBLIC ENEMY #1
(REVELATION 12:1-17)

The problem of evil and suffering in the world has been a dilemma that theologians and philosophers have debated for centuries. It goes something like this: "If God is good and all-powerful, then why is there so much evil and suffering in the world?" The Christian usually phrases it like this: "God, Why did you let this happen to me?" Too often in these discussions, God gets no credit for the good things we receive, and gets all the blame for the bad things that happen. Guess who usually gets off scot free in these discussions? The Devil. I believe that he is the perpetrator of more evil and suffering than any other single individual. Some, however, doubt his existence for which I am sure he is grateful. Revelation chapter 12 gives us a great deal of information about the Devil and his character and activities.

I. The Woman in Hiding   12:1-6   (The Scene is on Earth.)

John calls this a "sign". He lets you know when he is speaking symbolically. This is *not* a literal woman. She is symbolic.

   A. Her Appearance   12:1

John draws on the symbolism throughout the Scriptures in his writings. This picture is similar to that found in Genesis 37:9-10 which was Joseph's dream about his brothers who became the nation of Israel.

   B. Her Child   12:4-5

Before we can establish the woman's identity, we must first establish the identity of her son. This is a reference back to Psalm 2:7-9 which is a Psalm of David. The New Testament interprets who this Psalm speaks of in Acts 4:25-27. It is a clear reference to Jesus Christ. Several suggestions have been given concerning the woman's identity.

   1. "The Church": However, the church didn't give birth to Christ. It was the other way around.

   2. "Mary": However this is a "sign" and not a literal woman. This woman is to be protected during the Tribulation. This rules out Mary.

58

3. "Mary Baker Eddy": Founder of Christian Science who claimed to be this woman. She is no longer alive. (Strauss, 228)

4. "Israel": In Isa. 9:6 "us" refers to Israel. Other Scriptures also point out that Jesus was a son of Israel. (Heb. 7:14/ Rom. 9:4-5/ Micah 5:2-3/ Isa. 66:7-8) It seems clear that the woman in Revelation chapter 12 who will be persecuted by Satan is the nation of Israel.

C. Her Enemy 12:3-4

"Sign" indicates that this is *not* a literal dragon, but a symbol. It is a symbol of Satan. The color "red" speaks of his bloodthirsty cruelty. Jesus said Satan was a murderer from the beginning. The fact that John sees a "dragon" speaks of his ferocity. He is vicious. The fact that he has seven heads and ten horns identifies him with the beast of Daniel chapter 7 and Revelation 13:1. The diadems which he wears speaks of his great power. One third of the stars fall at his command.

"Stars" are sometimes used symbolically to speak of angels (cf. Rev. 9:1-2/ Job 38:7). Satan was once an angel named Lucifer who fell due to pride and ambition (Isa. 14:12-14/ Ezek. 28:12-15). Apparently in his fall he took one third of the angelic realm with him (Jude 6/ 2 Peter 2:4).

D. Her Divine Protection 12:6

Here again we see reference to 1260 days or 3 and 1/2 years. This appears to be the last half of the Tribulation. During this time Satan will do his best to persecute the Jews and to annihilate them from the earth.

II. The War in Heaven 12:7-12 (The Scene is in Heaven.)

The scene now moves to heaven. There is a warfare going on in the heavenlies even now for world supremacy. Apparently at the halfway mark of the Tribulation, Satan loses that war and the earth becomes his only sphere of activity. He will then be free to unleash his full anger toward the earth.

A. An Angelic Army 12:7

The battle is fought between two angelic armies. Michael means "Who is like God?" (Lucifer said, "I will be like God." Isa. 14:12) Michael is called an Archangel and also appears in Dan. 10:13,21/ 12:1/ and Jude 9. He is the leader of God's angelic army.

B. An Angry Adversary 12:7-12

Satan is angry because he is defeated and his doom is sealed.

1. His Access to Heaven 12:7-8

Satan apparently has access to heaven in some sense. In Job's day he appeared there to wrongly accuse Job (1:6/ 2:1-6). In Luke 10:18 Jesus foresaw Satan losing this battle.

2. His Titles 12:9-10

Dragon=for his viciousness

Serpent of Old=This identifies him with the Garden of Eden.

Devil="slanderer" Jesus called him the "father of lies" (John 8:44).

Satan="adversary" He is our enemy. 1 Peter 5:8

Deceiver of the whole world=2 Cor. 4:4/ 11:14

Accuser of the brethren=Christians have an advocate (1 John 2:1-2).

3. His Undoing 12:11

John gives three keys to victory over Satan.

    a. The blood of the lamb. There's Power in the Blood (1 John 1:7).

    b. The word of their testimony. Their witness. Evangelism

    c. Their death. Tertullian, an early church father said, "The blood of the martyrs is the seed of the church." Satan will think he is winning when he kills them, but it will be his undoing.

4. His Anger 12:12

"Rejoice O heavens"

"Woe to the earth"

Why?

    a. because earth is now Satan's only sphere

    b. because he knows his time is limited to 1260 days

III. The War on Earth 12:13-17   (The Scene is on Earth.)

The scene now switches back to the earth and Satan centers his attack on Israel.

A. Satanic Anti-Semitism

Anti-Semitism is of the Devil. It is satanically inspired. Haman, Pharaoh, Antiochus Epiphanes, Hitler, Stalin, Anti-Christ, all are inspired by Satan. Why does he so hate the Jewish people and want to destroy them?

    1. Because they are special to God (Even now in their unbelief, cf. Rom. 9-11)

    2. Because of the Abrahamic Covenant (Gen. 12:1-3). God has made them some eternal promises. If Satan can obliterate them, then he can thwart God's plan.

B. Sovereign Protection

God delivers them on "eagles wings" (cf. Ex. 19:4).

"her place" God has provided a place of protection for them.

"time, times, and half a time" cf. Dan. 4:16, 3 and 1/2 years or the last half of the Tribulation.

"nourished" Like Elijah at Cherith, Israel will be divinely nourished.

"flood" could be a literal flood or a reference to invading armies.

"earth" could be a literal earthquake or some other means of divine protection.

"the testimony of Jesus" Being thwarted in his attempt to exterminate Israel, Anti-Christ will turn His attention to believers, Christ followers (v. 17).

According to verse 17, this will be the worst wave of persecution to ever sweep the earth (cf. Dan. 12:1/ Matt. 24:15-22). It will be directed against both Christians and Jews, many of whom will have become Christians because of this persecution. It will be a war. Perhaps it would be wise to decide *now* whose side you want to be on. Choose wisely.

LESSON 16
THE MARK OF THE BEAST
(REVELATION 13:1-18)

In Revelation chapters 12 and 13 we are introduced to the Evil Trinity. Satan is the great imitator of God. Just like God, he has his own trinity. Satan, who said "I will be like the Most High God," is anti-God. The Beast, the great imitator of Christ is anti-Christ. The False Prophet who leads people to follow the Beast is anti-Holy Spirit. Chapter 13 describes two wild beasts who will come on the scene during the Tribulation. They are men, but from God's perspective they are wild, ravenous beasts.

I. The Beast from the Sea   13:1-10   (A Political Ruler)

God is going to turn this world over to Satan. He will never be able to make the accusation "You never gave me a chance." He wants to be like God and rule and he will have his chance and fail miserably.

   A. His Description   13:1-2

He arises out of the "sea." The "sea" in prophetic literature often refers to the Gentile nations (cf. Dan. 7:2). The beast described here is similar in appearance to the beast in Daniel 7:7-8. He is identified with the Roman Empire and is seen as arising from the ashes of that empire (cf. Dan. 7:19-26). Political leaders have tried throughout the centuries to revive the Roman Empire. Charlemagne, The Roman Catholic Church, Napoleon, Kaiser Wilhelm, Hitler, and Mussolini all tried to unite Europe and failed. The Beast will succeed. Keep your eyes on the EEC, the European Economic Community. They presently have 12 member nations and are trying to unite with a common economy and currency.

"10 horns" = 10 kings   cf. Rev. 17:12

"7 heads" = 7 mountains and 7 kings   cf. Rev. 17:9-10

"blasphemous" = 1) Making oneself equal with God

                    2) slandering and taking God's name in vain

v. 2 cf. Daniel 7

"dragon" His authority comes from Satan (Rev. 12:9).

B. His <u>Deceit</u> 13:3-4

He has a fatal <u>wound</u>. 13:3,12,14, and 17:8

He has a false <u>resurrection</u>. 13:3 It is false because only Jesus can raise the dead (John 5:21-29/ 11:25-26). The world will not accept Jesus' resurrection, but they will accept this fake resurrection. The world will fall for the "big lie" and accept his lies (2 Thess. 2:8-12). The word "<u>worship</u>" is used 5 times in this chapter. This is what Satan truly desires.

C. His <u>Defiance</u> 13:5-8a

    1. Through his <u>words</u> 13:5-6

    2. Through his <u>deeds</u> 13:7

He becomes a world leader through military might.

He overcomes the saints through bloody persecution.

He beheads many (Rev. 20:4).

He receives the worship of men.

    3. His <u>limitation</u> 13:5

God limits his reign of terror to 42 months.

D. God's <u>Faithful</u> <u>Saints</u> 13:8b-10

Lamb's book of life   Is your name written there?

        Is it possible to know? cf. 1 John 5:13

"foundation of the world"   This means we were chosen.

"an ear to hear"   Are you receptive to God's Word?

II. The <u>Beast</u> from the <u>Earth</u> 13:11-18   (A <u>Religious</u> Ruler)

Man is incurably <u>religious</u>. In Revelation 17 we read about the apostate church that helps Anti-Christ come to power. He will have a great prophet who helps him in his deceit.

A. His <u>Description</u> 13:11

He acts like a <u>lamb</u>. (He imitates Christ. cf. Rev. 5:6)

He speaks like a <u>dragon</u>. (His message is from Satan.)

Matt. 7:15/ 24:24

B. His <u>Deceit</u> 13:12-15

Satan is *not* against religion. He inspires much of it. He is against <u>personal</u> <u>faith</u> in Christ. The False Prophet deceives the multitudes by:

    1. Directing the <u>worship</u> of the Beast.

His purpose is to promote the worship of the Beast.

(cf. the Holy Spirit, John 16:14)

    2. Doing <u>Miracles</u>.

Satan has supernatural powers. He imitates the miracles of the two witnesses. This comes about after their death. Compare his activities to that of the Egyptian sorcerers who imitated the miracles of Moses in Pharaoh's court.

3. Building an <u>Idol</u> that talks.

Jesus said that false prophets would arise (Matt. 24:24). The test of a prophet in Deuteronomy 13:1-4 is *not* his miracles, but his <u>message</u>. That is true today. The technology exists today to build such a lifelike idol. It did not exist in John's day.

C. His <u>Device</u>   13:16-18   (for controlling humanity)

The Mark of the Beast. It will be his "pledge of allegiance."

    1. It is <u>Universal</u>. v.16

    2. It is <u>Visible</u>. v. 16

    3. It is <u>Essential</u>. v. 17

    4. It is a <u>Number</u>. v. 18

It is easier to identify people with numbers (Social Security, Driver's License, Telephone). The technology exists today to build such a system that could identify each person, and give vital up to the minute information about them.

THE MARK VI PERSONAL IDENTITY VERIFIER

Biometric Technology Today newsletter tells us that one company, PIDEAC, has recently gone into large-scale production of its Mark VI Personal Identity Verifier. The article says:

This hand geometry verification device is unusual in that it does not require users to place their hands within posts or grooves located on the reading area. Instead, the company has developed a technique which allows the hand to be placed anywhere within the reading area. Both hands can be enrolled in the system in case of injury to one in the future.

The student of Bible prophecy will not only be interested in the name of this device, but in the fact that its developers have decided to record both hands in case of injury. The Bible may well have been foretelling just such a precaution when it referred to "marking" the right hand or forehead.

There are some other interesting features of the new Mark VI system as well. Not only can the device be used for ID verification, but it can be programmed with access time restrictions, with the names and employee numbers of authorized users, and with time and attendance records for payroll purposes.

This Mark VI system will be priced at about $6,300 - not an exorbitant price when you consider the time-saving security measures it provides. But PIDEAC is currently testing a simpler and smaller device for low- or medium- security use which measures the length of only four fingers. These devices would cost less than $1,000. Besides their obvious uses, these smaller devices could be mounted on the dashboards of cars as antitheft devices or provide access and security in restricted parking areas.

(From: <u>Racing Toward the Mark of the Beast</u> by Peter and Paul Lalonde. p.76-77)

5. It is Eternally <u>Fatal</u>. 14:9-11

It will present a clear choice. Those who receive the "mark" will know what they are doing.

Conclusion:

We do not wait for Anti-Christ. We wait for Jesus Christ. In the meantime we must be aware that we live in a world that is "anti-Christian" (1 John 2:15-17). We must not allow ourselves to be conformed to this world's way of thinking. Our thoughts, attitudes, and actions must be based on the Word of God. Examine the conclusion of the Anti-Christ and his False Prophet in Revelation 19:11-16, 19-20. Don't follow a loser. Follow the biggest winner of all time, Jesus Christ the Lord.

LESSON 17
SIX POSTCARDS FROM THE FUTURE
(REVELATION 14:1-20)

In Revelation chapter 14 we find six brief messages from the future. Because they are graphic we could call them snapshots, because they are messages we could call them letters, because they are brief we will call them postcards. Everyone likes receiving postcards from exotic locations. These are from some of the most exotic.

I. The First Postcard: From the <u>Millennium</u>   14:1-5

This postcard pictures the group of 144,000 saved <u>Jews</u> that we met back in chapter 7. It apparently comes from the Millennium since they are gathered on Mount Zion with the Lord Jesus. Their song of praise and thanksgiving reaches up to the throne room of Heaven (v. 3).

A. They are <u>standing</u>.   14:1

They are standing because they are <u>victorious</u>. All that the Beast could do did not knock them down.

B. They are <u>sealed</u>.   14:1

They are victorious because they were <u>sealed</u> by God (7:3). Christians are sealed by the <u>Holy Spirit</u> (Eph. 1:13/ 4:30).

C. They are <u>singing</u>.   14:2-3

They have been through a lot, but they haven't lost their <u>song</u>. (Don't let the bitter experiences of life take away your song.)

D. They are <u>special</u>.   14:3

They are given a "new song" which no one could learn but them.

E. They are <u>separated</u>.   14:4

They had "not been defiled with women." They were "chaste." This means they were completely <u>separated</u> unto the God they served. This is *not* a commentary on <u>women</u>, or <u>marriage</u>. Marriage is "honorable" (Heb. 13:4). This may mean that they were <u>literally</u> unmarried virgins, or it could refer to their separation from the <u>religion</u> of the Beast. They

66

had not <u>compromised</u> with his false religion. Their devotion is evident since they follow the Lamb.

"Firstfruits" is the promise of <u>more</u> to come. Because of their devotion to Christ, many more will follow.

F. They are <u>sincere</u>.   14:5

There was "no lie" in their mouths. There was no falsehood. This especially refers to their <u>message</u>. They remained true to their message about Christ. They did *not* compromise.

II. The Second Postcard: From the <u>Sky</u>   14:6-7

A. The <u>Messenger</u>   14:6

The message is delivered by "another <u>angel</u>." This is one of five mentioned in this chapter. During the church age God has entrusted His Gospel message to <u>people</u>. With so many Christians martyred during the Tribulation God will use an <u>angel</u> preaching from the sky to deliver this gospel. People will not be able to say they did not know. Everyone will hear (cf. Matt. 24:14).

B. The <u>Message</u>   14:7

This refers to God as both <u>Judge</u> and <u>Creator</u>. It is a reminder to all those who will live during the Tribulation and be pressured to worship the Beast. God is Judge, so <u>fear</u> Him. He is Creator, so <u>worship</u> Him, and *not* the Beast. (I am amazed at how many times that Revelation refers to God as the <u>Creator</u>. It is a great reminder to all of us who live in a day when men have refused to give God the <u>credit</u> for His creation.) This is God's final call.

III. The Third Postcard: From <u>Babylon</u>   14:8

The word "fallen" is "prophetic aorist." It refers to something in the <u>future</u>, yet it is stated as though it happened in the <u>past</u>. It is a sounding out of judgment. It is stated in the past tense because it is very <u>certain</u> to happen.

A. The <u>Identity</u> of Babylon the Great

The destruction of <u>Religious</u> Babylon is described in Revelation 17. It is the apostate church which has amalgamated all of world religion. It helps the Beast come to power during the Tribulation.

The destruction of <u>Economic</u> Babylon is described in Revelation 18. It refers to the economic system which the Beast uses to control the world.

B. The <u>Iniquity</u> of Babylon the Great

Her iniquity is so great that it affects "all the nations." "Her immorality" is probably a figure of speech for her <u>false</u> <u>religion</u>. In Exodus 34:14-16 <u>idolatry</u> is referred to as immorality. Christians are warned to separate themselves from false religion (James 4:4).

IV. The Fourth Postcard: From <u>Hell</u>   14:9-11

This postcard is not a pretty picture. It is not for the faint of heart.

A. The <u>Inhabitants</u> of Hell   14:9

Those who worshipped the <u>Beast</u> or received his <u>mark</u>. Because of the intense persecution in that day, a person cannot <u>casually</u> call himself a Christian. It would cost his life.

B. The <u>Intensity</u> of Hell   14:10

Notice the description that the Holy Spirit gives of Hell. It is characterized by the "<u>wrath</u> of God." God's wrath will be "full strength" or undiluted. There will be *no* <u>mercy</u> or <u>grace</u> or <u>kindness</u> mixed into it. It is described as a real <u>place</u> where real <u>people</u> will be "tormented with fire and brimstone" as God and the angels look on.

C. The <u>Eternity</u> of Hell   14:11

Hell is as <u>eternal</u> as Heaven. They will be tormented "forever and ever." There will not be a <u>pause</u> in their torment. "They have no rest day and night."

Remember: These people, just like us, will be warned about the terrible consequences of rejecting Christ. They have only themselves to blame. If you have never personally decided to receive Christ as your Savior and publicly confess Him (Rom. 10:9), even though you have not yet received the mark of the Beast, your sin is no different than theirs (John 3:36). *Why not confess Him as your Savior today?*

V. The Fifth Postcard: From <u>Heaven</u>   14:12-13

I am so glad that God includes this postcard. I wish I had a real postcard from Heaven to show you.

A. The <u>Perseverance</u> of the Saints   14:12

The Devil has his crowd, but Christ has His. These people persist in following Christ even when everything is against them. They "keep the commandments of God" *not* the Beast, and they do not lose "their faith in Jesus." God <u>preserves</u> them and <u>delivers</u> them safely to Heaven.

B. The <u>Pleasure</u> of the Saints   14:13

This reference to the Tribulation saints is true of *all* genuine believers.

1. They are <u>rejoicing</u>. "blessed" = happy

2. They are <u>resting</u>. "they...rest from their labors" (Notice the contrast with those who receive the mark of the Beast in verse 11.)

3. They are <u>rewarded</u>. "their deeds follow with them" (cf. 2 Cor. 5:10)

Matthew 6:20, 21 "But lay up for yourselves treasures in heaven, where neither moth nor rust destroys, and where thieves do not break in or steal; for where your treasure is, there will your heart be also." (Jesus)

VI. The Sixth Postcard: From the <u>Clouds</u>   14:14-20

It is a postcard from Glory where preparations are being made for <u>Armageddon</u> and the judgment to follow.

A. The <u>Son</u> of <u>Man</u>   14:14 (Jesus)

He is called the "son of man" (cf. Rev. 1:13).

He is sitting on a <u>cloud</u> (cf. Acts 1:9-11/ Matt. 24:30).

He is pictured with a golden <u>crown</u>. It is a "stephanos" which is a victor's crown. He has conquered <u>death</u> and the <u>devil</u> and deserves to win this world. Jesus is the ultimate Victor.

He has a sharp <u>sickle</u>. He is reaping judgment on the earth. It is preparation for Armageddon.

B. The <u>Sickle</u> of <u>Judgment</u>   14:14 ff.

The <u>angels</u> are the reapers (Matt. 13:41-42/ 49-50/ 24:31).

Verse 20 seems to be a reference to the Battle of Armageddon. The Megiddo valley where the Battle of Armageddon will be fought drains into the Jordan system allowing sufficient mileage to fulfill this prediction (<u>Revelation</u>, Ryrie, 93).

LESSON 18
THE SONG OF VICTORY
(REVELATION 15:1-8)

Throughout history men have sung to commemorate their victories. Our national anthem is an example. The Song of Moses commemorated God's victory over the Egyptians. In Revelation the saints will sing their song of victory *before* the final battle is fought. The outcome is sure and we are on the winning side.

I. The Seven Angels of God's Justice   15:1, 5-7

These seven angels carry the seven plagues in the seven bowls we will read about in chapter 16.

    A. The Finality of the Seven Plagues   15:1

They are "the last." We are happy to see the end of God's wrath. God's wrath "is finished" in these plagues. God's wrath is never too much or too little it is always just sufficient.

    B. The Wrath of the Seven Plagues   15:1,7

Verse 1 and verse 7 describe these last seven judgments as being characterized by "God's wrath." God is merciful, loving, and kind (Jonah 4:2/ Ex. 34:6-7), but He can be pushed too far by nations (Gen. 6:3), and by individuals (Prov. 29:1). "It is a terrifying thing to fall into the hands of the living God." Heb. 10:31

    C. The Righteousness of the Seven Plagues   15:5-6

These plagues are not vindictive. They are vindicative (Ryrie, Revelation, 94). God will vindicate His righteousness or justice. God will vindicate His word. God will vindicate His followers. These plagues are righteous because they proceed from God's Temple. The fact that God is just is precisely what many people do *not* like. (cf. Gen. 18:18-25, esp. 25/ Rom. 12:19)

II. The Sea of Glass   15:2

This is the scene around the throne of God.

    A. The Sea

This is *not* an ordinary sea. It is figurative ("as it were"). Glass is <u>reflective</u>. This sea is designed to reflect the <u>glory</u> of God. "Mixed with fire." The fire speaks of divine <u>judgment</u> which proceeds from the <u>holiness</u> of God. Some have suggested that since the saints are standing on it, that this sea represents God's faithfulness in keeping His own.

B. The Singers

They are holding harps. They are singing with accompaniment. Some people believe it is not scriptural to sing with musical accompaniment. They will be singing this way in heaven. These are tribulation saints who are said to be "victorious from the beast."

How could they be victorious when they were martyred or killed by the Beast? They were victorious because they did not give in. God enabled them to keep the faith even unto death. (cf. 1 Cor. 15:55-57/ James 1:12)

III. The <u>Song</u> of Redemption   15:3-4

A. What it <u>Commemorates</u>.

In Exodus 14 God rescued the Israelites from the clutches of Pharaoh's army by drowning them all in the Red Sea. In Exodus 15 we read the song of deliverance and redemption that Moses and his people sang to commemorate God's victory over their enemies. They had been rescued from slavery in Egypt by the Passover and the Red Sea. The Song of the <u>Lamb</u> commemorates an even greater victory. It is a victory over <u>sin</u> and its eternal <u>consequences</u>. It was wrought by Calvary, and the Resurrection. It is also wrought by these judgments of the end times. That is why we sing "Victory in Jesus."

"Victory in Jesus"

O victory in Jesus, my Savior, forever,
He sought me and bought me with His redeeming blood,
He loved me ere I knew him, and all my love is due him,
He plunged me to victory, beneath the cleansing flood.

B. What it says about <u>God</u>.

   1. His <u>Person</u>: He is …

   Almighty

   Righteous

   True

   King (Sovereignty)

   Holy

   2. His <u>Works</u>: They are …

   Great

   Marvelous

   Revealing

C. What it says about <u>People</u>. (What should our response be to Him?)

   1. We should <u>fear</u> the Lord.

There is not much fear of God today. There is not much reverence for who He is.

   2. We should <u>glorify</u> His name.

Today, many people curse His name and use it in vain.

   3. We should <u>worship</u> Him.

In the Ten Commandments, people were told to set aside the Sabbath Day and keep it holy. It was a day of worship. Today, most have neglected to give God His day of worship. People find many excuses not to worship. Most find time to play, time to shop, time to work, time to rest, but no time to worship God. "The nations will come." Even our nation must stand before Him.

IV. The Smoke of God's Glory   15:8

We do not really understand or appreciate the glory and the holiness of God today. The Old Testament was full of God's glory.

Exodus 19:18 = <u>Sinai</u>

Exodus 40:34 = The <u>Tabernacle</u>

1 Kings 8:10-11 = Solomon's <u>Temple</u>

Isaiah 6:1-5 = Isaiah's <u>Vision</u>

Ezekiel 10-11 = The Glory <u>Departed</u>

Ezekiel 43 = The Glory Will <u>Return</u>

Wherever God is, there is <u>Glory</u>. The Bible says that you and I have fallen short of God's glory (Rom. 3:23) because we are all sinners. John said that the disciples beheld God's glory in the person of Jesus Christ (John 1:14).

   God's judgment may seem severe to some. Salvation is in three tenses:

   1. In the <u>Past</u>: We have been saved from the <u>Penalty</u> of Sin. <u>Justification</u>

   2. In the <u>Present</u>: We are being saved from the <u>Power</u> of Sin. <u>Sanctification</u>

   3. In the <u>Future</u>: We shall be saved from the <u>Presence</u> of Sin. <u>Glorification</u>

This severe judgment is what it takes to complete our salvation. It is the extreme surgery that is necessary to restore this planet to God's dominion and to free it from sin and Satan. There is no such thing as freedom without bloodshed. That is why Christ shed His blood so you could be freed from the Penalty, Power, and eventually even the Presence of sin.

LESSON 19
THE SUPER BOWL JUDGMENTS
(REVELATION 16:1-21)

Chapter 16 describes in detail the third series of judgments delivered in the book of Revelation. The 7 Seal judgments are found in chapter 6. The 7 Trumpet judgments are found in chapters 8 and 9. The 7 Bowl judgments are found in chapter 16. These judgments delivered near the end of the Tribulation bring us to the final events before the Second Coming of Christ which are the destruction of Babylon, and the Battle of Armageddon.

I. The First Bowl: <u>Bleeding</u> <u>Sores</u>   16:1-2

These are the same seven angels that we met in 15:1. Now they come to deliver their judgments to unrepentant humanity.

    A. The <u>Realm</u> of the Judgment

"into the earth"

    B. The <u>Result</u> of the Judgment

"malignant sores" The Greek word is "helkos." It is the same word that the Greek translation of the Old Testament uses to refer to the "boils" which were used in the ten plagues against Egypt (Ex. 9:9-11) (Walvoord, 232). This judgment is directed specifically toward mankind, and *only* toward those who <u>worship</u> the image of the beast. God will not abide idolatry, the transferring of the glory He rightfully deserves to another god or person. This is clearly seen in the first two commandments (Ex. 20:3-6). This situation is really very similar to Pharaoh and Moses. It involves a <u>king</u> who refused to acknowledge God's sovereignty.

Notice: the Beast cannot <u>cure</u> his worshippers or <u>protect</u> them from these plagues which apparently occur in rapid succession.

II. The Second Bowl: <u>Bloody</u> <u>Seas</u>   16:3

    A. The <u>Realm</u> of the Judgment

"into the sea"

This is similar to the second trumpet which affected 1/3 of the sea and its creatures.

B. The <u>Result</u> of the Judgment

The sea "became blood" and "every living thing in the sea died." In the Ten Plagues of Egypt the Nile became blood and all the fish died (Ex. 7:20-25).

Question: Is it literal blood?

Answer: It is inconsequential. If Jesus can turn the water into wine, then He can turn water into blood or something just as loathsome (LaHaye, 215).

III. The Third Bowl: <u>Bloody</u> <u>Springs</u>   16:4-7

Mankind has been affected, the sea, and now the <u>fresh</u> <u>water</u> supply will be affected as the rivers and springs become blood.

A. The <u>Realm</u> of the Judgment

"into the rivers and springs of water"

B. The <u>Result</u> of the Judgment

"they became blood"

C. The <u>Reason</u> for the Judgment

"they poured out the blood of the saints"

The angel who delivers this judgment declares the righteousness of God. God is righteous and just in His judgments against these people because they poured out the blood of the saints. In other words, because they were bloodthirsty, God has given them blood to drink. God is perfectly just. The saints are worthy of rest and reward (Rev. 14:13). The wicked are worthy of divine judgment.

Dr. John Walvoord of Dallas Theological Seminary says this is "a universal testimony to all men that God will avenge His martyred saints" (Walvoord, 234).

IV. The Fourth Bowl: <u>Blazing</u> <u>Sun</u>   16:8-9

A. The <u>Realm</u> of the Judgment

"upon the sun"

B. The <u>Result</u> of the Judgment

"men were scorched with fierce heat"

Literally, "the men." This may refer to the beast worshippers. If so, then it implies that the saints will be <u>protected</u> from these plagues. The Fourth Trumpet resulted in a darkening of the sun, but this judgment increases the suns intensity.

"They blasphemed the name of God...and they did not repent" (cf. 9:20-21). Here we see the <u>hardness</u> of the human heart. Some say that if they saw the rapture take place, and saw the Beast and his mark and his image, *then* they would believe, but that is *not* what the Bible teaches. If a person refuses to repent *now*, then he will not repent when God is evidently at work.

V. The Fifth Bowl: <u>Blinding</u> <u>Darkness</u>   16:10-11

A. The <u>Realm</u> of the Judgment

"upon the throne of the Beast"

This judgment primarily affects his kingdom. Since he claims to be God, God will prove how impotent the Beast really is.

B. The Results of the Judgment

"his kingdom became darkened"

This is reminiscent of the ninth plague of Egypt. The prophet Amos said "The day of the Lord is a day of darkness and not light" (Amos 5:18). This judgment will make it evident to all the world that the Beast is *not* in control. This plague does not cause him or any of his people to repent. They blaspheme God and stubbornly refuse to repent. This indicates that whenever people reject Christ, it is *not* an intellectual problem, rather, it is a hardness of heart and a love for sin (LaHaye, 219). God gives them justice. They prefer the devil's darkness to God's light so God gives them all darkness (John 3:19-20). Hell is also a place of darkness (Matt. 22:13).

VI. The Sixth Bowl: Barrier Removed   16:12-16

A. The Realm of the Judgment

"upon the Great River, the Euphrates"

This ancient river is 1800 miles long. In places it is 3600 feet wide and 30 feet deep (Phillips, 195). This river formed the eastern boundary of the Roman Empire and the prophesied eastern boundary of Israel (Gen. 15:18). More than likely, it is a boundary to the Beast's empire. It has formed a natural barrier between East and West. This judgment dries up a natural boundary. It will be judgment on Babylon.

B. The Result of the Judgment

"its water dried up"

This will cause Iraq and Babylon to become a desert. It will remove the Beast's natural defense. God is notorious for drying up rivers to let people pass over (Josh. 3). The kings of the East seems to refer to the oriental rulers who will rebel against the Beast. These nations may include Japan, China, India, and a vast array of smaller nations (Walvoord, 236). Verses 13,14, and 16 indicate that God will allow the armies of these nations to be gathered to Armageddon. This will apparently be a major military campaign described in Daniel 11:40-45. It seems that this vast world empire put together by the Beast disintegrates and the armies come to Armageddon to fight. During the final battle of this campaign they all unite in their opposition to the Returning Christ (Rev. 19). It will be their final challenge to God's sovereignty.

C. The Recommendation of the Judgment

"Behold, I am coming like a thief" (cf. 2 Pet. 3:10 / 1 Thess. 5:2-6).

"stay awake" This warning is to Tribulation saints. It is a warning to vigilance. Those who are not ready will suffer loss.

"keep your garments clean" This is a warning not to compromise, even if the Beast offers peace and pardon to those he has persecuted if they will join his army. This also refers to righteousness expressed in their testimony and lifestyle.

VII. The Seventh Bowl: <u>Brutal</u> <u>Natural</u> <u>Disasters</u>   16:17-21

A. The <u>Realm</u> of the Judgment

"upon the air"

B. The <u>Results</u> of the Judgment

"lightning...thunder" These are harbingers of a coming <u>storm</u>.

"a great earthquake"

This is described as the greatest earthquake ever. This is a <u>literal</u> earthquake. It affects "the great city." This city is probably the city referred to in this verse and the subject of the next two chapters, <u>Babylon</u>. There are many good reasons to believe that Babylon will be <u>rebuilt</u> and perhaps used as the Final Capital of the Beast. Perhaps this is the judgment referred to in chapter 18.

"huge hailstones" They each weigh a talent which was 100-125 pounds. It is judgment comparable to Sodom and Gomorrah. These men continue to <u>blaspheme</u> God and receive the Biblical judgment for this, being stoned to death (Lev. 24:16) (Wiersbe, 611).

Summary:

In the midst of all this talk of judgment to come, perhaps we need to be reminded *why* this book of Revelation was written.

1. To answer the question: "What on earth is God doing for Heaven's sake?"

In the midst of suffering this is an often asked question. "How can God allow suffering and sin to continue?" "Why does evil seem to be in control?" "Is it really worth it to live for Christ?" John's original audience was being tortured and killed for confessing Christ. They needed this assurance that living for Christ was ultimately worthwhile.

2. To answer the question: "How will Christ regain control of this world?"

He will win it by conquest. World leaders will not gladly hand it over to Him.

3. To encourage believers to remain faithful during times of persecution.

It is a promise of future vindication and reward for every believer.

4. It is a serious and gracious warning to every unbeliever.

Revelation 1:3 is a promise to those who hear and heed the message of this prophecy.

LESSON 20
THE FALL OF WORLD RELIGION
(REVELATION 17:1-18)

The Church is described in Scripture as a pure bride. In Revelation 19:7-9 there is an invitation to the "marriage supper of the Lamb." She is clothed in fine linen "bright and clean; for the fine linen is the righteous acts of the saints." In Ephesians 5:25-27 the church is described as a bride of Christ who is made clean by His redemptive work. His work on her behalf has made her "holy and blameless." In Revelation chapter 17 we are presented with the stark contrast of a brash and impure harlot who rides atop the back of the Beast. This woman depicts world religion and especially a false church which actually persecutes genuine believers. In this chapter this impure and devilish creation will receive her just reward from God.

I. The <u>Description</u> of the Woman   17:1-7

  A. The <u>Great</u> <u>Harlot</u>

    1. "a woman" 17:3

Religions and philosophies are often pictured in Scripture as <u>women</u> (e.g.. Prov. 7 & 8, Eph. 5:25-27, Rev. 12). This woman is *not* a literal woman. She is symbolic of an apostate <u>church</u> and amalgamated <u>religion</u>. The fact that she is *symbolic* is seen in the fact that she is riding on the back of the *symbolic* "beast" which we met in chapter 13. She is "mystery." The fact that she is described as a harlot indicates that she uses her influence to <u>seduce</u> many people away from a right relationship with God. Dr. John Walvoord says, "The concept of spiritual adultery is frequently used in describing the apostasy of Israel" (Walvoord, 244) (cf. Ezek. 16:15, 20-21/ Hosea 4:11-12/ Prov. 9). On the other hand the church is presented in the Scripture as a pure <u>bride</u> (2 Cor. 11:2). Believers are warned against spiritual <u>adultery</u> (James 4:4). There are always those in the organized church who want to make it more like the <u>world</u>, who want the world's <u>approval</u>.

    2. "many waters"   17:1

This seems to be a reference to her <u>influence</u> over many multitudes of people. According to verse 15 she will have influence over "peoples and multitudes and nations and tongues."

3. "acts of immorality"   17:2

This "woman" craves political power and will do anything to get it. The immorality here seems to be a compromise of Christian <u>truth</u> to achieve worldly <u>ambitions</u>, probably even so far as to changing gods.

4. "kings of the earth"   17:2

This is an impure union between <u>church</u> (religion) and <u>state</u>.

5. "clothed in purple and scarlet"   17:4

Verse 4 pictures the harlot as <u>wealthy</u> and dressed in the colors of <u>royalty</u>. But all of this does not cover up her vileness as represented in the cup which she drinks.

6. "upon her forehead a name"   17:5

"<u>Babylon</u> the Great" This name identifies her with a <u>city</u>, possibly a rebuilt Babylon or a code name for Rome.

"The Mother of Harlots" From early times Satan has been busy <u>perverting</u> the true faith and drawing multitudes into <u>false</u> religious systems which the Scripture would call "harlots."

"The subject of Babylon in the Scripture is one of the prominent themes of the Bible beginning in Genesis 10 where the city of Babel is first mentioned, with continued references throughout the Scriptures climaxing here in the book of Revelation. From these various passages, it becomes clear that Babylon in Scripture is the name for a great system of religious error. Babylon is actually a counterfeit or pseudo religion which plagued Israel in the Old Testament as well as the church in the New Testament, and which, subsequent to apostolic days, has had a tremendous influence in moving the church from biblical simplicity to apostate confusion. In keeping with the satanic principle of offering a poor substitute for God's perfect plan, Babylon is the source of counterfeit religion sometimes in the form of pseudo Christianity, sometimes in the form of pagan religion. Its most confusing form, however, is found in Romanism." (Walvoord, 246)

B. The <u>Scarlet</u> <u>Beast</u>   17:3

The woman is riding on the scarlet beast which indicates that she has <u>power</u> over it. This beast which has seven heads and ten horns is described in detail in chapter 13. It is a reference to the <u>political</u> empire of the Anti-Christ. The Apostate church or united world religion of that day will lend its <u>influence</u> to the Beast for <u>political</u> power. Together they will wage war on the true saints of God and get drunk on the blood of the saints (17:6). The Beast will no doubt use her influence to help his rapid rise to power.

II. The <u>Domination</u> of the Woman   17:8-15

This woman will seemingly dominate the beast and the world for a time.

A. The Seven <u>Heads</u> of the Beast   17:8-11

This beast will rise so <u>suddenly</u> from the ashes of the past ("*was* and is not and will come" v.8) that people will gasp in "wonder," especially those whose names have "*not* been written in the book of life."

    1. A Location   17:9

The woman sits on "many waters" in verse 1, indicating her influence on vast multitudes of people. She is seated on the "beast" in verse 3, indicating her political power and influence on governmental decisions. In verse 9 she is seated on "seven mountains," which seems to indicate the seat or the base of her ecclesiastical or religious power. This seems to be a very clear reference to Rome. Ovid wrote, "But Rome looks around on the whole globe from her seven mountains, the seat of empire and abode of the Gods." (McGee p.52).

    2. A Legacy   17:10

These seven heads are said to be seven kings or kingdoms.

"Five have fallen." This seems to indicate five different world empires that have fallen in the past. (Possibly: Egypt, Assyria, Babylon, Persia, and Greece). "One is." This seems to be a reference to the Roman Empire of John's day.

"The other has not yet come." This refers to a future kingdom which will be the Beast's empire or the forerunner of his empire which will be a revived Roman Empire.

B. The Ten <u>Horns</u> of the Beast   17:12-13

This seems to refer to the <u>political</u> makeup of this kingdom. It will be a political confederation made up of 10 <u>nations</u>. This seems to correspond to the image represented in Daniel 2 by the 10 "<u>toes</u>" and in Daniel 7 by the beast with 10 "<u>horns</u>." It is still <u>future</u> since John says they "have not yet received a kingdom." It will be a <u>short-lived</u> alliance since it will last only "one hour."

C. The <u>Doom</u> of the Beast   17:14

Apparently these 10 kings will pledge their allegiance to the Anti-Christ and together they will attempt to wage open warfare with the <u>Lamb</u>. They will be <u>defeated</u>. Their political power is <u>satanic</u> in its origin and is destined for Hell.

III. The <u>Destruction</u> of the Woman   17:16-18

What is seen in this chapter is a <u>political</u> empire and a world <u>religion</u> using each other for their personal gains. They enter into an unholy alliance that results in the worldwide persecution of the saints and the spread of the Beast's evil empire.

A. Her <u>Doom</u>   17:16

The Beast and his allies make an alliance with the Harlot of World Religion in order to use her influence to rule the world. After their power is <u>secure</u> their true feelings for her will be revealed. They "hate the harlot." They despise her and will turn on her killing those associated with her ("eating her flesh") and taking all of her wealth ("desolate and naked"). Here we see the danger of <u>church</u> (religion) and <u>state</u> joined together.

B. Her <u>Destroyer</u>   17:17

This passage makes it clear that "*God* has put it in their hearts to execute *His* purpose." These kings are only accomplishing <u>God's</u> will. They are merely God's unwilling <u>servants</u>. God is rewarding the harlot who has so thoughtlessly spilled the blood of His saints (cf. 17:6). So it will be for all those who make themselves the enemies of God.

Summary:

The Great Harlot of Revelation 17 seems to be the apostate church and possibly an amalgamation of all major world religions. It is a truly ecumenical church that is unable to save anyone, not even itself.

It is good to know that Christianity is not really a religion. It is a relationship with Jesus Christ (cf. 1 John 5:12). It is the only relationship in the world that can save you from the terrifying judgments of the Tribulation period, and ultimately from Hell itself.

LESSON 21
COMMERCIAL BABYLON DESTROYED
(REVELATION 18:1-24)

Babylon involves both a city and a system. Revelation chapter 17 refers to *Religious* Babylon. It is apostate religion. It is a *religious system* that will involve an amalgamation of world religions. It is associated with Rome and her seven mountains. It will enable the Beast to come to power. Revelation chapter 18 refers to *Commercial* and *Political* Babylon. It is an *economic system* that will enable the Beast to control and enslave the world. While it may be associated with Rome, it seems very likely that it may involve a rebuilt city of Babylon.

I. The <u>Announcement</u> by the Angel   18:1-3   (cf. 16:19)

A. The Announcement comes from a bright, powerful <u>angel</u>.

B. "Fallen" This is the prophetic perfect tense which demonstrates that this judgment is yet <u>future</u>, but it is <u>certain</u>. The angel repeats it for emphasis.

Once the great Roman Empire was the most powerful on earth. Yet, that great empire sank down to failure. What were the causes? Historian Edward Gibbon, in his story of *The Decline and Fall of the Roman Empire, gives* these five reasons for that failure:

1. The rapid increase of *divorce*; the undermining of the dignity and sanctity of the home, which is the basis of human society.

2. Higher and higher taxes and the *spending* of public monies.

3. The mad craze for *pleasure*; sports becoming every year more exciting and more brutal.

4. The building of gigantic armaments, when the real enemy was within: the *decadence* of the people.

5. The decay of *religion*--fading into mere form, losing touch with life and becoming impotent to warn and guide the people.

Does any of the above sound familiar?   (<u>The Preacher's Illustration Service</u>, 1988)

C. Babylon is <u>demonically</u> inspired. "a dwelling place of demons." v.2

D. Babylon is <u>unfaithful</u>, <u>immoral</u>, <u>idolatrous</u>. v.3

E. Babylon is very <u>seductive</u>. It is possible for even <u>Christians</u> to be seduced by her wealth and her luxuries, and immoralities.

Will Babylon be rebuilt? John calls it a "<u>city</u>" 8 times.

Could Babylon merely be a code word for <u>Rome</u>? Possibly, cf. 1 Peter 5:13

"The destruction of Babylon according to Jeremiah 51:8 was to be sudden. This is confirmed by Revelation 18:17-19. As far as the physical city of Babylon was concerned, this was not true of ancient Babylon as it continued for many years after its political downfall. Further, it is pointed out that the prophecy of Isaiah 13:19-22, indicates that the destruction of Babylon would be in the day of the Lord. Hence, it is held that Babylon will be rebuilt and then destroyed by Christ at His second coming.

Others identify Babylon as Rome, the seat of the apostate church as described by the seven mountains of 17:9 and also the political city as elsewhere described. It is possible that Rome might be the ecclesiastical capital and rebuilt Babylon the political and commercial capital. It is also conceivable that Rome might be the capital in the first half of the last seven years and Babylon in the second half - in the world empire phase. " (Walvoord, 262)

II. The <u>Warning</u> to Believers   18:4-8

A. The <u>Exhortation</u>   "Come out of her, my people"   18:4

The primary application is to believers living during the <u>Tribulation</u>, however, it applies to believers of every time. It is a relevant application. "Do not compromise with Satan's world system."

B. The <u>Explanation</u>   18:4

There are two reasons given for obeying the Lord's command.

1. "That you may not participate in her <u>sins</u>"

Her sins are listed later in this chapter as immorality, idolatry, materialism, greed, and slavery, not to mention the murder of many saints.

"God has remembered her iniquities" v.5

2. "That you may not receive of her <u>plagues</u>"

Verse 8 describes that in "one day" her judgment will come in the form of pestilence, mourning, famine, and fire.

"Pay her back even as she has paid" v.6   God is just!

"To the <u>degree</u> that she has glorified herself and lived sensuously, to the *same* degree give her torment and mourning" v.7

C. The <u>Examples</u>

1. Lot (Seduced by Sodom) Genesis 19

2. Demas ("loved this present world") (cf. 2 Tim. 4:10/ 2 Cor. 6:14-7:1/ 1 John 2:15-17)

III. The <u>Weeping</u> of Kings and Merchants   18:9-19

    A. The <u>Kings</u> Weep   18:9-10

The same kings who rejoiced in destroying <u>religious</u> Babylon in chapter 17 will weep and lament over the <u>commercial</u> Babylon of chapter 18. These political rulers will be sad to see this "queen" of commerce destroyed. They "stand at a distance" and look on at her destruction. They experience a sense of "<u>fear</u>" because it is a forerunner of their own imminent judgment. Babylon is described by the Kings as a "strong city." It will apparently be well fortified just as the Babylon of ancient times was the most well-defensed city of its time.

"In one hour" is a <u>theme</u> of this chapter (vv.10, 17, 19) that emphasizes the <u>swiftness</u> and <u>suddenness</u> of the destruction of this city. The kings are surprised and the merchants are horrified.

    B. The <u>Merchants</u> Weep   18:11-19

They do not weep for the city so much as they weep for <u>themselves</u>, "because no one buys their cargoes any more." They are upset because they have lost their best market. The <u>kings</u> weep because they can no longer trust in her <u>military</u> might. The <u>merchants</u> weep because they can no longer trust in her <u>wealth</u>.

This is a materialistic system. Notice that these goods are all <u>luxury</u> items. The rich and wealthy will have plenty of luxuries during this Tribulation, while the poor cannot even buy bread (Rev. 6:5-6).

Where is your Treasure? Jesus said, "Do *not* lay up for yourselves *treasures upon earth*, where moth and rust destroy, and where thieves break in and steal, but lay up for yourselves *treasures in heaven*, where neither moth nor rust destroys, and where thieves do not break in or steal; for where your treasure is, there will your heart be also." Matt. 6:19-21

How does a person lay up treasure in Heaven?

IV. The <u>Vindication</u> of God and His Saints   18:20-24

The Saints are told *not* to participate in this evil system of Babylon (v.4), and they are told to rejoice in its destruction (v.20). It would be hard to rejoice in Babylon's destruction if that is where your <u>valuable</u> things were invested. Believers were supposed to be excluded from buying or selling in Babylon without the mark of the Beast.

    A. The <u>Saints</u> are Vindicated   18:20-21

This is the judgment that is requested by the <u>saints</u> in Revelation 6:9-11. Babylon slew the saints and now God slays Babylon thereby showing that the faith of the <u>saints</u> was well placed. Her destruction is complete and utter like a millstone that is cast into the sea never to be seen again.

    B. <u>God</u> is Vindicated   18:22-24

Babylon <u>deceived</u> the nations (v. 23/ cf. 12:9), and Babylon <u>killed</u> the saints (v. 24/ cf. 13:7). Divine judgment demonstrates that God is <u>really</u> God and is a <u>just</u> judge. No one violates His laws and gets away with it. God is righteous and He punishes those who persecute His own.

Will the city of Babylon be rebuilt? It is *already* being rebuilt.

"It is a cloudless September summer night, and the moon casts its shining image on the banks of the gentle Euphrates River. Thousands of guests and dignitaries walk by torch light to Babylon's Procession Street and enter the city from the north. Instructed to line the streets along the massive walls, the guests obediently follow orders. When the audience is in place, the dark-eyed man in charge nods, and the procession begins.

Rows and rows of soldiers parade in, dressed in Babylonian tunics and carrying swords, spears, and shields. Interspersed among the ranks of soldiers are groups of musicians playing harps, horns, and drums. Clusters of children carry palm branches, and runners bear bowls of incense. Then come soldiers and still more soldiers in a seemingly endless line of men and weapons. After the procession, the guests attend a ceremony paying tribute to Ishtar, the mother goddess of Babylon.

Have I just described a scene of pagan worship from the time of Daniel? Perhaps, but it is also exactly what I witnessed when I returned to Babylon in 1988 for the second International Babylon Festival held under the patronage of Saddam Hussein." (Charles H. Dyer, <u>The Rise of Babylon</u>, 16, 17)

Conclusion:

1. It might be difficult for some of us to understand rejoicing at the destruction of a city of so many people. It is easy for us to debate this, however, the believers in John's day were undergoing violent persecution just like the saints in the Tribulation will face. We've never really suffered persecution and lost our possessions, our families, and our lives unjustly. We're afraid of losing our tax-exempt status. In that day we will gladly rejoice in the complete destruction of Babylon.

2. Where is your citizenship? Is it in Babylon, or in Heaven? Are you planning your life like you were going to live down here forever, or like you were going to live in Heaven forever? Do you get your joy from the things on earth or the things of heaven? Remember God's exhortation to believers, "Come out of her, my people."

3. Where is your treasure? Is it on earth or in Heaven? If you were to lose all of your material possessions in one day like Job, what would you have left? Answer: Only what you have invested in Heaven.

What do you have invested in Heaven right now?

LESSON 22
THE SECOND COMING
(REVELATION 19:1-21)

There is a difference between the *Rapture* and the *Second Coming* of Christ. In the *Rapture*, Christ comes *for* His Church (1 Thess. 4:13-18), in the *Second Coming* He comes *with* His Church (Rev. 19:14). In the *Rapture* He comes to take His Church to Heaven, in the *Second Coming* He comes to set up His Kingdom on earth. The Pre-tribulational position holds that the *Rapture* takes place *prior* to the Tribulation and the *Second Coming* takes place seven years later *after* the Tribulation. Here in Revelation 19, John describes the Second Coming of Christ following the bloody years of the Tribulation when the Beast is still in power.

I. Christ's Coming <u>Applauded</u> in <u>Heaven</u>   19:1-10

At the end of chapter 18 (18:20), the saints are told to rejoice at Babylon's destruction and its implications. Chapter 19 records their (and our) exuberant rejoicing.

   A. The <u>Worship</u> of the Lamb   19:1-6

These verses describe a great praise and worship service in Heaven just prior to the Lord's victorious Second Coming. It is a passage that is filled with great enthusiasm and elation and lifts our hearts to Heaven.

   1. The Four <u>Hallelujah's</u>   (The Hallelujah Chorus)

"A great multitude" This praise chorus is sung by a great chorus of redeemed <u>saints</u> and elect <u>angels</u>. Notice that there will be a "great" <u>population</u> in Heaven.

"Hallelujah" This word is used only in this chapter in the New Testament. It is a Hebrew word which means "<u>Praise</u> <u>the</u> <u>Lord</u>."

"Amen" This word means "<u>so</u> <u>be</u> <u>it</u>," or "<u>true</u>." It is used to affirm the <u>truth</u> of a statement, or a person's wholehearted <u>agreement</u> with a statement. You had better get used to hearing and speaking these two words on earth because you will be using them in Heaven.

   2. The <u>Reason</u> for His Praise

      a. Because He has <u>delivered</u> us   v.1

    b. Because He has <u>judged</u> our enemies   v. 2

    c. Because He has assumed His <u>rightful</u> place as <u>King</u>   v. 6

B. The <u>Wedding</u> of the Lamb   19:7-10

This is a wedding announcement. It is a time for rejoicing. It has been a very long engagement.

    1. The Bridegroom   19:7

Usually the glory goes to the Bride, but here it goes to the Groom ("give glory to Him"). The marriage is announced in His name ("the marriage of the Lamb"). The time "has come." There is no more delay.

    2. The Bride   19:7b-8   (cf. Eph. 5:25-27/ 2 Cor. 11:2)

The Bride is the Church. She has "made herself ready."

Everyone always wants to know what the Bride wore. She is wearing "fine linen, bright and clean." These garments are described as "the righteous acts of the saints." The Church is the Bride because of what Christ did. The wedding gown is because of what we do. What have you been doing to adorn the wedding gown of the Church? (McGee, Vol. 2, 68)

"Though marriage customs varied in the ancient world, usually there were three major aspects: (1) The marriage contract was often consummated by the parents when the parties to the marriage were still children and not ready to assume adult responsibility. The payment of a suitable dowry was often a feature of the contract. When consummated, the contract meant that the couple were legally married, (2) At a later time when a couple had reached a suitable age, the second step in the wedding took place. This was a ceremony in which the bridegroom accompanied by his friends would go to the house of the bride and escort her to his home. This is the background of the parable of the virgins in Matthew 25:1-13. (3) Then the bridegroom would bring his bride to his home and the marriage supper, to which guests were invited, would take place. It was such a wedding feast that Christ attended at Cana as recorded in John 2:1-12.

The marriage symbolism is beautifully fulfilled in the relationship of Christ to His church. The wedding contract is consummated at the time the church is redeemed. Every true Christian is joined to Christ in a legal marriage. When Christ comes for His church at the rapture, the second phase of the wedding is fulfilled, namely, the Bridegroom goes to receive His bride. The third phase then follows, that is, the wedding feast. Here it is significant to note that the bride is already the wife of the Lamb, that is the bridegroom has already come for His bride prior to His second coming described in 19:11-16. That which is here announced is not the wedding union but the wedding feast. This has been variously interpreted as relating to the wonderful fellowship in heaven following the rapture or to the millennium itself. Of primary importance at this point, however, is the order of events. The third phase of the wedding is about to take place, namely, the feast, which presumes the earlier rapture of the bride. The translation would be much improved in verse 7 if it would read "for the marriage feast of the Lamb is come." (Walvoord, 271)

3. The <u>Blessing</u>   19:9

A blessing (beatitude) is pronounced on the guests. Who are the guests? Not the <u>Bride</u>, no Bride has to be invited to her own wedding. Not the <u>unsaved</u>, they have no part. Answer, they are redeemed people who are *not* a part of the church, i.e. the <u>Old Testament</u> saints and <u>Tribulation</u> saints (cf. John 3:29). The marriage supper *is* in the <u>Millennial</u> Age. The marriage takes place in <u>Heaven</u>, but the Marriage supper takes place on <u>Earth</u>. It is a 1,000 year long honeymoon (McGee, Vol 2, 69).

4. The <u>Blunder</u>   19:10

<u>John</u> makes a blunder at this point. He is overwhelmed by this revelation and worships the one who imparts it. He is <u>corrected</u> by the messenger. We are to worship God alone, not men or <u>angels</u>.

II. Christ's Coming <u>Accomplished</u> on <u>Earth</u>   19:11-21

Christ's glorious appearing, His Second Coming in power and great glory is the most exciting event in Bible prophecy, and it is the event along with Christ's first coming, around which all of history is arranged. History is moving toward this climactic event. Scripture is clear in its promise of Christ's return (cf. Zech. 13:3-4/ Acts 1:9-11/ Matt. 24:27-31). The literal nature of Christ's Second Coming to earth is a clear emphasis in the New Testament. Any person, group, or teaching that minimizes its importance is highly questionable.

A. His <u>Appearance</u> Reveals His <u>Right</u> to <u>Rule</u>   19:11-16

He is regal ("white horse"), and He is "<u>righteous</u>." The purpose of His coming is to <u>judge</u> and wage <u>war</u> (v.11). He is the <u>sole</u> ruler of the universe and wears "many diadems" (v. 12). He comes wearing the blood-stained garments of battle (v. 13). He comes with <u>angelic</u> and <u>human</u> armies, but we're just along for the ride because our Champion does all the fighting. His weapon for judging is a <u>sharp</u> <u>sword</u> which proceeds from His mouth. It is the <u>word</u> of God (Heb. 4:12/ Eph. 6:17). He will hold the nations accountable to His Word. He is given three names in this passage. One is unstated in verse 12, one is the "Word of God" in verse 13, and one is "King of Kings, and Lord of Lords" in verse 16 (cf. Psalm 2).

B. His <u>Arrangements</u> Reveals His <u>Coming Victory</u>   19:17-18

The arrangements for His arrival involve a huge <u>supper</u> for the birds.

The location of this supper seems to be <u>Armageddon</u> (cf. Rev. 16:16).

It is ironic that men who chose to live in the flesh, will have their flesh eaten by the birds. There are *two* suppers in this chapter, the marriage supper of the Lamb, and this supper for the birds.

Which supper would you rather attend?

C. His <u>Arrival</u> Reveals His <u>Power</u> to <u>Judge</u>   19:19-21

Apparently, these armies have come together to fight each other (Rev. 16:12-16). The Beast's evil <u>empire</u> has broken down. There is bloody <u>world</u> <u>war</u>. The battlefield where the armies have converged is <u>Armageddon</u>. As they prepare to fight each other, suddenly Christ appears in the Sky. The armies choose to unite in opposition to Christ. The Anti-Christ and the world resist Christ to the bloody end.

The Devil who inspires the Beast and the False Prophet knows his final hour has come, yet he refuses to surrender. Human life has no value to him. The <u>Beast</u> and <u>False</u> <u>Prophet</u> are captured and thrown alive into the "<u>lake</u> <u>of</u> <u>fire</u>." They are still there <u>1,000</u> years later (Rev. 20:10,15). <u>Satan</u> is cast into the bottomless pit for <u>1,000</u> years (Rev. 20:1-3). The rest of those who oppose the Second Coming of Christ are killed with the "sword" which proceeds from Jesus' mouth. It is a violent scene, but those who spurn God's grace, must experience His wrath.

"For God so loved the world, that He gave His only begotten Son, that whoever believes in Him should not perish, but have eternal life. For God did not send the Son into the world to judge the world, but that the world should be saved through Him. He who believes in Him is not judged; he who does not believe has been judged already, because he has not believed in the name of the only begotten son of God." John 3:16-18

LESSON 23
THE MILLENNIUM
(REVELATION 20:1-10)

"Joy to the world, the Lord has come." We all enjoy singing this wonderful hymn around Christmas time. What you may not realize is that this is not a Christmas hymn, but a Millennial hymn. It does not speak of Christ's first coming, but of His second coming. Throughout the years men have longed for a golden era marked by peace and prosperity. Today's passage, Revelation 20:1-10, speaks about this time. It is also one of the most controversial passages in Scripture among believers. I'm not sure why because it reads so clearly.

Millennium comes from two Latin words, "mille" which means a thousand, and "annum" which means, year. It is also called the Messianic Kingdom. It is the great theme of the Old Testament prophets. It is the message that Christ came preaching. "The *kingdom* of heaven is at hand."

There are three basic views concerning the Millennium. The *Amillennial* position believes that there will be no literal thousand year reign of Christ on the earth. The *Postmillennial* position states that the church will get stronger and stronger, and the world will get better and better, and the church will usher in the thousand year kingdom. The *Premillennial* position states that there will be a literal thousand year reign on this earth, and that Christ will personally come to this earth before this time to set up His kingdom. (cf. Appendix 6)

I. The <u>Commencement</u> of the Millennium   20:1-3

In Revelation chapter 19 we see the battle of Armageddon, the fate of the Beast and the False Prophet (19:20), and the fate of their armies (19:21). In Revelation 20 we begin by seeing the fate of Satan (20:1-3).

A. <u>Initial</u> <u>Act</u> of the Millennium   (The <u>Binding</u> of Satan)

These verses indicate that at some future time Satan will be <u>imprisoned</u> by God. God will send an angel to bind him with a "chain" and cast him into the "abyss" or the "bottomless pit." This "abyss" will then be "shut" and "sealed" for "a thousand years" (v. 2,3). Four different names are given for <u>Satan</u> here, "the dragon," "the serpent of old," "the devil," and "Satan."

There could be no peaceful earth with Satan loose. This will be a time of great rejoicing.

Imagine that a terrorist who lived in your neighborhood and relentlessly terrorized your family, your friends, your neighbors, looted and plundered almost at will. He tricked people out of money, murdered, raped, etc. Suddenly he was caught and put in prison. Everyone would rejoice.

The Amillennialist believes that the church age that we are now living in is the millennium, and that Satan has already been bound. Dr. Grey used to say, "He must be on a very long chain" (Wiersbe, 619). Satan is active today. He is *not* yet bound (1 Pet. 5:8). Verse 3 says that he will be "loosed for a little while." Why? Dr. Louis Sperry Chafer, founder of Dallas Theological Seminary said, "If you can tell me why God let him loose in the first place, I will tell you why God let him loose the second time" (McGee, Vol. 2, 74). Nevertheless, during the Millennial Kingdom, the Devil will not be able to tempt, murder, lie, kill, steal, or destroy.

B. Names for the Millennium

Dr. Harold Willmington lists eight different names that the Bible gives for the Millennial Kingdom (Willmington, 207).

1. The World to Come   Heb. 2:5

2. The Kingdom of Heaven   Matt. 5:10

3. The Kingdom of God   Mark 1:14

4. The Last Day   John 6:40

5. The Regeneration   Matt. 19:28

6. The Times of Refreshing   Acts 3:19

7. The Restitution of All Things   Acts 3:21

8. The Day of Christ   1 Cor. 1:8/ 5:5/ 2 Cor. 1:14/ Phil. 1:6/ 2:16

Understanding this will help you to read these passages with new eyes.

II. The Christ of the Millennium   20:4

Verse 4 speaks of "thrones" and "reigning with Christ." This is the 1,000 year reign of Christ on earth. It would be beneficial to *underline* every time "thousand years" is mentioned in Revelation 20:1--10. It is mentioned *six* times. Throughout the book, John gives us numbers. There are seven churches. He names all seven. There are 12,000 Jews from 12 different tribes that all receive the seal of God on them. God protects the woman mentioned in Revelation 12:6 for 1,260 days. These are *not* just symbolic numbers. They are literal. God mentions the "thousand year" reign of Christ *six* times to emphasize that it is literal. Christ will literally rule and reign on this earth from His capital city of Jerusalem for one thousand peaceful and prosperous years.

This is the Kingdom which was:

A. Foretold by the Prophets

Isa. 9:6-7/ 11:2-9/ Dan. 2:34-35, 44-45

B. Preached and Offered by Jesus

Matt. 4:17

C. Expected by the Disciples

Acts 1:3-7

D. Promised in the Covenants

    1. Abrahamic Covenant   Gen. 12:1-3

    2. Palestinian Covenant   Deut. 28

    3. Davidic Covenant   2 Sam. 7:12f/ Lk. 2:32-33

    4. New Covenant   Jer. 31:31-34/ 33:14-18

In order for these prophecies to be fulfilled Jesus *must* return and reign as sovereign over this earth.

E. Understood by the Early Church

Henry Alford, noted Greek scholar, made this comment concerning the early church's literal interpretation of this passage:

"Those who lived next to the Apostles and the whole Church for 300 years, understood them in the plain literal sense; and it is a strange sight in these days to see expositors who are among the first in reverence of antiquity, complacently casting aside the most cogent instance of consensus which primitive antiquity presents. As regards the text itself, no legitimate treatment of it will extort what is known as the spiritual interpretation now in fashion" (Pentecost, Things to Come, 491). Even Augustine who popularized Amillennialism believed the 1,000 years was literal (Walvoord, 294).

III. The Citizens of the Millennium   20:4-6

A. The Savior will be Ruling.   (19:15)

We will "reign with Christ" (v.4). He has come back to receive His rightful place of authority over all (cf. Phil. 2:9-11/ 1 Cor. 15:24,25).

B. The Saints will be Resurrected.   20:4-6

The Tribulation saints "came to life." They are resurrected after the Tribulation and will reign with Christ. There are several resurrections mentioned in the Scriptures. It is a Resurrection Parade.

    1. Christ "firstfruits" 1 Cor. 15:20

    2. The Church 1 Thess. 4:13-18

    This is the Rapture prior to the Tribulation.

    3. The Tribulation Saints Rev. 20:4

    4. The Old Testament Saints? Dan. 12:2

    Some believe that they will be raised at the same time as the Tribulation saints. Others believe they will be resurrected when the Church is resurrected at the Rapture.

C. The Saints will be Reigning 20:4-6

These believers are resurrected and on the scene for a very important purpose. We will be reigning with Christ. There are three groups of believers mentioned in verse 4.

1. Those seated on Thrones

I believe this is the church. The Scriptures make it clear that the church will have positions of authority in Christ's Kingdom (cf. Lk. 19:17/ 1 Cor. 6:2/ 2 Tim. 2:12).

2. Those beheaded for Jesus

These are the martyred Tribulation saints.

3. Those not receiving the Mark of the Beast

These are Tribulation saints who died for other reasons.

These three groups will have "thrones," "reign with Christ," and are called "priests of God." They will be princely priests, and priestly princes.

D. The Survivors will Enter the Kingdom

Though this passage does not state it, some believers will survive the Tribulation and enter the Millennium. Apparently this will include the 144,000 Jews who are mentioned in chapters 7 and 14. It must also include a number of Gentile believers from many nations who rejected the Anti-Christ and trusted in Jesus. Daniel 12:11-13 indicates that some will survive this terrible time.

E. The Sinners will be Resurrected   20:5-6

After the "thousand years" are over there will be another resurrection. It will *not* be a resurrection to life, but a resurrection to death. The first resurrection (mentioned in verse 4) leads to life. The second resurrection (mentioned in verse 5) leads to the "second death" (cf. 20:14-15). One thousand years separates these two resurrections.

IV. The Conditions of the Millennium   20:6

John writes that those who go into the Millennium are "blessed and holy." "Blessed" means happy. Happiness and Holiness go together. The world has it backwards today. People look for happiness in sin and unholiness. The reason there is so little happiness is because there is so little holiness. People will be living by the precepts of the Sermon on the Mount. Whatever else it will be, it will be characterized by these two words, "blessed and holy." Some Old Testament passages that describe this period are Isaiah 11 and 60, and Jeremiah 31.

V. The Close of the Millennium   20:7-10

As wonderful as the Millennium will be, it is *not* Heaven. These verses state that Satan will be released from the "abyss" at the end of the "thousand years." He will set out to once again "deceive the nations." The world will be populated with mortal men and women just like us who still have a sin nature, and still must make a personal decision to trust Christ for their eternal salvation. Many of these people will *not* want to trust Christ, even though they will submit to His government. Even after one thousand years of the greatest peace and prosperity that humanity will ever know, they will still want to rebel against Christ. No doubt, they will be tired of His iron rod. Verse 9 describes a future battle, a second Armageddon, that will occur in which Christ will answer once and for all the question of who has the right to rule. Satan's final doom is described as the "lake of fire" where he will be "tormented day and night forever and ever."

This final rebellion reveals two very important facts: 1) Man is still wicked, and needs to be redeemed. We have a sin nature. Whether a person is born in the ghetto, or in a palace, whether to good parents, or rotten parents, whether in the Old Testament times, or in the Church Age, or in the Millennium, man is a sinner who left to himself will choose to act independently of God and live a sinful and rebellious lifestyle. 2) Satan has not <u>reformed</u>. After a great defeat and a thousand years to think about who God is, he and his fallen angels still choose to rebel against God. He still desires to <u>deceive</u> the nations. He is beyond redemption.

Conclusion:

The real question for you is where will you be during the Millennium? Will you be ruling and reigning with Christ and enjoying the blessings of happiness and holiness, peace and prosperity, or will you be awaiting the second resurrection which leads to the "second death?" You do have a choice.

LESSON 24
THE GREAT WHITE THRONE JUDGMENT
(REVELATION 20:7-15)

Revelation 20:7-15 discusses the final destiny of Satan, and all those who refuse to accept Jesus Christ as Savior. This passage grabs the attention of both the saved and the unsaved. It is a vindication for Christians and a warning for non-Christians. It speaks of mankind's final rebellion and God's final word. So buckle up and prepare for a wild ride.

I. Mankind's Final <u>Defiance</u>   20:7-9

  A. Mankind's <u>Paradise</u>   20:7

"The thousand years," refers to the completion of the Millennial Kingdom. It is a golden age for humanity. There is worldwide peace, worldwide economic stability, incredible health care, an end to violent crime, no need for missionaries, an end of poverty, widespread prosperity, no need for prisons, mental institutions, alcoholism, drug addiction, no rapists, and no abortion clinics. Righteousness reigns.

  B. Satan's <u>Plans</u>   20:8

Today Christians have three enemies: the <u>world</u>, the <u>flesh</u>, and the <u>devil</u>. During the Millennium there will be only one, the <u>flesh</u>, since the devil will be chained in the "abyss," and Christ will be ruling this world system. When he is released at the close of the thousand years, he will once again set about to "deceive the nations." People who have no <u>experience</u> of listening to his lies, and have not <u>personally</u> trusted Christ will be deceived.

If you have never trusted Christ as your personal Savior, believing in *Him* and *Him alone* to forgive you of all your sins, then *you* are also being deceived by Satan. Consider Satan's destiny.

  C. God's <u>Penalty</u>   20:9

Satan leads his *last* attack on God and His people. He is risking everything as he attacks God's beloved city. Human life means nothing to him. He is not worried about losing his army. This ill advised army of rebels will experience a second <u>Armageddon</u>. They are destroyed in a moment, "fire came down from heaven and devoured them." Those who refuse to learn the lessons of history are doomed to repeat them.

II. Satan's Final <u>Destiny</u>   20:10

A. The Truth about <u>Satan</u>

Satan does *not* live in <u>hell</u>. 1 Pet. 5:8

Satan will *not* be the <u>first</u> in hell.   "the beast and the false prophet"

Satan *is* a <u>deceiver</u>. He does not go around advertising his existence.

Satan *is* as <u>real</u> as you and I.

Satan does *not* want you to believe the truth about <u>hell</u>.

B. The Truth about <u>Hell</u>   "the lake of fire"

1. It is <u>eternal</u>. "day and night forever and ever"

2. It is a place of <u>torment</u>. "tormented"

3. It is a place of <u>consciousness</u>. cf. Luke 16:19-31

4. It is a place of <u>memories</u> of past opportunities. cf. Luke 16:19-31

5. It is a place of <u>hopelessness</u>. There is no escape. cf. Luke 16:19-31

6. It is a place with <u>degrees</u> of punishment. cf. Rev. 20:12

7. It is a place of <u>loneliness</u>.

Why is there a need for Hell?

1. Hell is necessary because of God's <u>righteousness</u>. He must judge sin.

2. Hell is necessary because of man's <u>responsibility</u>. We are not robots or helpless victims. We are able to make choices. God sends no one to hell. A person sends himself, when he rejects Jesus.

3. Hell is necessary because of the awfulness of <u>sin</u>. If we could see sin like God sees it, we would understand. (Wiersbe, 621)

III. Mankind's Final <u>Damnation</u>   20:11-15

The Great White Throne Judgment is lost mankind's final condemnation. "White" represents the <u>holy</u>, righteousness character of Christ. "Throne" reminds us that this judge has *absolute sovereignty*. His decisions cannot be appealed. It is a throne of *absolute justice*, if that is what you really want. Today, we are invited to approach a "throne of grace" (Heb. 4:15-16).

A. The Righteous <u>Judge</u>   20:11

Who is this righteous judge? It is <u>Jesus</u> (cf. John 5:22, 25-29). The One who <u>redeems</u>, is the One who has the right to <u>rule</u>. He is the same One who was worthy to open the "book" (Rev. 5:2). Earth and Heaven flee from His holy stare. "No place is found for them." There is no place to <u>hide</u>. What a sobering thought.

B. The Resurrection of the <u>Lost</u>   20:12-13

Only <u>unbelievers</u> will be present at this judgment. No Christians will be present. The purpose of this judgment is to establish a person's <u>guilt</u> and their *degree of punishment* ("according to their deeds"). All unbelievers will be there "great and small." The dead will be resurrected since "death and Hades" will give up their dead. They will be resurrected in <u>bodies</u> suitable to eternal punishment.

Reincarnation is a farce invented by the devil to deceive men and women into thinking they will receive another chance after this life. The unsaved will not be reincarnated, they will be resurrected (Heb. 9:27).

C. The Rightful Basis for <u>Judgment</u>   20:12-13

The "books were opened." Books are so black and white. What books? 1) The Word of God, the Bible (John 12:48), is the <u>standard</u> by which all are judged. 2) The second book is the <u>record</u> of our works ("according to their deeds"). This book determines the degree of punishment or sentencing. No one is saved by works, but many want to be judged by them, and will be in one sense. God will judge sins of <u>commission</u>, and sins of <u>omission</u> (Rom. 2:16). 3) The "Book of <u>Life</u>" (v. 15) will be their final appeal. It contains the names of all who are saved (Rev. 3:5/ 20:15/ 21:27). Every person, no matter how bad who realized his sin and his inability to save himself, and humbly, like the thief on the cross, asked Jesus to save him will be listed in the "book of life."

Do You Know If Your Name Is Written There?

It Is Possible To Know (cf. 1 John 5:12, 13).

D. The Reality of <u>Hell</u>   20:14-15

"Death" claims the <u>material</u> part of man. "Hades" claims the <u>immaterial</u> part of man. Jesus holds the keys of <u>Hades</u> and <u>death</u> (Rev. 1:18). He has authority over both of them. Death will ultimately be destroyed (1 Cor. 15:54-56). The "second death" is mentioned in 20:6. It refers to <u>eternal</u> death. Someone said "Born once, die twice. Born twice, die once" (cf. John 3:7). Listen to the way <u>Jesus</u> described hell (Matt. 3:12/ 5:22/ 8:12/ 13:42/ 18:8/   Mark 9:48).

Imagine the sinking feeling in the pit of your stomach as you are approached by the strong angel. There is no place to hide. As he picks you up, you try to fight, but it is no use. There are screams, and wails. "No! This can't be the end." You are cast headlong into the yawning jaws of hell. No more happiness. No more mercy. No more love, or help, or hope, or rest, ever again.

Conclusion:

1. The Great White Throne Judgment is the *final* judgment before eternity begins.

2. Christ is *not* bluffing. The Bible is *not* bluffing. We are really accountable to the God who gave us life.

3. The Great White Throne is a throne of *absolute justice*. Today, however, you still stand before a "throne of grace" (Heb. 4:15-16).

If you have not already, please take advantage of the opportunity for forgiveness and salvation that God is offering today. If you would like to take advantage of Christ's gracious offer, then pray this prayer very sincerely from your heart.

"Dear Lord Jesus,

I know that I have sinned and done some wrong things and I cannot save myself. I believe you love me just like I am, and I believe you died for me on the cross, and then really rose from the dead on the third day.

Please come into my life and save me, right now. Forgive me of all my sin. Make me a part of your family. Give me a home in Heaven with you some day.   Amen

A Promise From Jesus

"Behold, I stand at the door (of your life) and knock if *anyone* hears my voice and opens the door, *I will come in* to him."   Revelation 3:20

If you have just prayed and asked Jesus to save you, please sign right here as a reminder of your commitment to Him, and then go and tell your Pastor, or a Christian friend about your decision.

_____ name

_____ date

LESSON 25
THE NEW JERUSALEM
(REVELATION 21:1-22:5)

In Revelation 21:1 through 22:5, John discusses and describes the New Jerusalem. It is the most specific discussion of Heaven that we have in the New Testament. What a source of encouragement it must have been for those early believers suffering under the heavy hand of persecution to read about the splendors that God has prepared for those who remain faithful to Him. What a motivation it must have been for them to "hang in there." Though they were *poor* on the earth, they would be *rich* in Heaven. Though they were *suffering* on earth, they would enjoy *health*, *peace*, and *prosperity* in Heaven. Though they were in the *minority* on earth, they would be the *majority* in Heaven. This wonderful assurance from God has given Christians throughout the centuries the faith to face life and death with courage even in the midst of overwhelming odds.

I. Some <u>Practicalities</u> of the New Jerusalem   21:1-8

This passage promises that in the future there will be a New <u>Heaven</u> and a New <u>Earth</u>. Other passages that also discuss these future plans are Isaiah 65:17, and 2 Peter 3:10-13. It could be a brand new <u>creation</u>, or it could be referring to a <u>recreation</u>. This means that it would be "new in character" (Wiersbe, 622/ Ryrie, <u>Revelation</u>, 119). These eight verses describe some things that will *not* be present in this "new world order" of Jesus Christ. There will be some very practical differences.

 A. No <u>Sea</u>   21:1-3

This must have been good news to John as he sat out there on the lonely Isle of Patmos, separated from friends and loved ones by the Mediterranean Sea on every side. In fact all that he could see on every side was that wide expanse of ocean that acted as a <u>barrier</u>.

The new earth will not have a <u>sea</u>. This does not that there will not be any water. No doubt there will be rivers, lakes, and streams. This does mean that there will be a different <u>climate</u> in the new earth.

 Notice several things about this recreated earth.

 1. It is <u>Holy</u>.   It is set apart unto God because God is there.

2. It is <u>Heavenly</u>.   It is "coming down out of heaven."

3. It is <u>Handsome</u>.   It is "made ready as a bride."

4. It is <u>Home</u>. "He shall dwell among them." God lives there and so do the saints of all ages. "Home" may be the most beautiful word there is to describe Heaven.

B. No <u>Sorrow</u>   21:4-7

1. The <u>Pain</u> is Gone.

There is so much pain here on earth. There is physical, mental, and emotional pain, but there will be none in Heaven. The <u>tears</u> will be wiped away. <u>Death</u> will cease. This mortal existence will be gone and so will the sufferings that go along with it (cf. Rev. 14:13).

2. The <u>Promise</u> is Given.

"I am making all things new." What a wonderful promise. Many of us have known the joy and excitement of moving into a new home we have built or bought with our limited resources. Imagine the excitement someday of moving into a brand new world tailor made for you with unlimited resources.

John got so excited at this point that he had to be reminded to "<u>write</u>." There are two requirements listed here for entrance.

One is to be <u>thirsty</u>. "I will give to the one who thirsts." You supply the thirst and He supplies the water. One is reminded of the discussion with the woman at the well in John 4 .

Second, you must be an <u>overcomer</u>. "He who overcomes shall inherit these things." I John 5:4-5 says that the key to overcoming is <u>believing</u> in Jesus. There are rewards for those who enter. They will have their thirst <u>satisfied</u>. The unsaved never have their thirst satisfied (cf. Luke 16:24). The saints will also be rewarded with intimate <u>fellowship</u> with God. "I will be his God, and he will be My son."

C. No <u>Sin</u>   21:8

Heaven wouldn't be heaven if <u>sin</u> were in the picture. Our founding fathers, the Pilgrims and the Puritans, were evangelical Christians who came to this New World in order to <u>escape</u> the sinful practices of the Old World and to worship God <u>freely</u>. But sin was *still* in the picture, and now, 400 years later, they would be looking for a new country if they were here today.

This list spells out the kind of people that will be <u>excluded</u> from Heaven. Of course, all who trust in Christ and receive forgiveness for these sins or any sin will be admitted. It includes "cowardly and unbelieving" people who were afraid to stand up for Christ publicly. "Sorcerers" refers to those who are involved in the occult, and those who use drugs. "Liars" are hypocrites who claim to be trusting in Jesus but really are not.

II. Some <u>Portraits</u> of the New Jerusalem   21:9-27

"Things which eye has not seen and ear has not heard, and which have not entered the heart of man, all that God has prepared for those who love Him" (1 Cor. 2:9). We can try to describe

Heaven, and we can look at some brief snapshots of Heaven, but it is impossible for a finite human mind to begin to imagine how wonderful a place God has prepared for us.

A. It is a <u>Precious</u> City.   21:9-11

This city which John saw was a "holy city" and is called "Jerusalem." It is said to possess the "glory of God." A city is not just buildings and streets. A city is people. This city is called "the bride, the wife of the Lamb." It is "<u>costly</u>" because it cost God a great price to obtain it.

B. It is a <u>Protected</u> City.   21:12-13

This city is surrounded by a "high <u>wall</u>" and has "twelve gates." Each gate is <u>guarded</u> by "twelve angels." These gates are named for the twelve tribes of Israel. There will be no fear of invasion here. It is secure.

C. It is a <u>Permanent</u> City.   21:14

This city is permanent. It has 12 foundation stones. Abraham was a nomad who lived in tents all of his life. He was "looking for a city" (Heb. 11:10). He wanted a <u>permanent</u> place to dwell. On each of these <u>foundation</u> stones is the name of an apostle. The church has been "built upon the *foundation* of the apostles and prophets, Christ Jesus Himself being the corner stone" (Eph. 2:20). It is interesting that only 12 apostles are included. That seems to do away with the notion of apostolic succession, or that there are any apostles living today. James, John's brother, was not replaced as an apostle after he was martyred by Herod (cf. Acts 12:1,2).

D. It is a <u>Prepared</u> City.   21:15-17

This city is not just thrown together. It is <u>planned</u> out and prepared. It is "<u>measured</u>." It is "laid out square." It seems to be a perfect cube. Jesus said, "I go to prepare a place for you" (John 14:1-6). Heaven is a prepared <u>place</u> for a prepared <u>people</u>.

Are you prepared? Have you made your reservation?

E. It is a <u>Plush</u> City.   21:18-21

This city is described as <u>elegant</u>, and <u>opulent</u>. Its walls are made of "jasper" (diamond, Walvoord, 104). Its streets are made of "gold." Its walls are decorated with all manner of "precious stones." It is beautiful. No <u>expense</u> has been spared. "Eye hath not seen, ear hath not heard" (1 Cor. 2:9).

F. It is a <u>Permeated</u> City.   21:22-23

There is no "temple" because <u>Jesus</u> is there. It has no sun or moon because the <u>glory</u> of God permeates it. "Its lamp is the Lamb." This city is permeated by the <u>presence</u> and the <u>glory</u> and the <u>love</u> of God.

G. It is a <u>Peaceful</u> City.   21:25

There is no night time there. The streets are <u>safe</u>. "Its gates shall never be closed." There will no need for locks in that celestial city. Locks are necessary because of sin. There will be no sin there. All the enemies of peace will have been done away forever.

H. It is a <u>Pure</u> City.   21:27

There is "nothing unclean" permitted in this city. There is no pornography, no HBO, no drugs, no liquor, no lying, no gossip, no slander, no adultery, no divorce, no greed, or anything that the Scripture considers to be <u>unclean</u>. There are no unsaved people there. There is "no one who practices abomination and lying...only those whose names are written in the Lamb's book of life." There will be plenty of people there who were saved out of horrible backgrounds, but only those who were genuinely saved and forgiven will be in Heaven. And they will no longer have a sin nature. It will be a great community in which to live.

III. Some <u>Perks</u> of the New Jerusalem   22:1-5

So far we have seen what things will be absent from the city, and what will be present in the city, but now we will see what the quality of life will be for those who reside in this New Jerusalem. Everything necessary for eternal <u>life</u> and eternal <u>happiness</u> will be there. It is not a place of *sordid* pleasures like some religions teach. Rather it is a place of *pure* pleasures and delights. It is a place of holiness and happiness. Inside, this city is like a beautiful and fragrant garden. This is the place Jesus promised to prepare for Christians (cf. John 14:2-3).

A. Eternal <u>Satisfaction</u>   22:1

Within every person is a <u>thirst</u> that cannot be satisfied by human means. Jesus said "Blessed are those who hunger and thirst after righteousness for they shall be satisfied" (Matt. 5:6). The "water of life" mentioned here in verse 1 has as its source "the throne of God and of the Lamb." In John 4:14, Jesus told the woman at the well "whoever drinks of the water that I shall give him shall never thirst."

This water satisfies not only the needs of the <u>body</u>, but the needs of the <u>soul</u>. There is an abundance of this water in Heaven, but none in the Lake of Fire. If you have an inner craving that has not been satisfied, only Jesus can satisfy it.

B. Eternal <u>Sustenance</u>   22:2

The "tree of life" was lost in <u>Genesis</u>, but it is regained in <u>Revelation</u>. Paradise Lost is Paradise Regained. It is called the "tree of life" because eating from it <u>results</u> in life. It is fruitful and desirable. Its fruit is never out of season. It bears "twelve kinds of fruit, yielding its fruit every month." It is sufficient to sustain eternal life and <u>health</u>.

C. Eternal <u>Paradise</u>   22:3

"And there shall no longer be any curse." After Adam and Eve sinned in the Garden of Eden, this world was placed under a curse. God said, "Cursed is the ground because of you; in toil you shall eat of it all the days of your life. Both thorns and thistles it shall grow for you and you shall eat the plants of the field; by the sweat of your face you shall eat bread" (Gen. 3:17-19). This curse, caused by mankind's <u>sin</u> and designed to point out mankind's <u>need</u> for God, resulted in disease, destruction, suffering, pain, and death. But in the New Heaven and New Earth there is *no more curse*. There is no cursed earth. There is no more sin nature, no more curse, and none of its results.

D. Eternal <u>Fellowship</u>   22:3-5

What will we do in Heaven for eternity? Sitting on a cloud and strumming on a harp forever is not really appealing to most people. God will have something for us to do. It will be something we <u>enjoy</u> doing and are well <u>equipped</u> to do. Heaven will *not* be a <u>boring</u> place. It will be above all a place of great <u>fellowship</u>. There are several aspects of this fellowship seen in these verses.

1. We Will <u>Serve</u> Him.   22:3

"And His bond-servants shall serve Him." I do not know in what capacity we will serve God and the Lamb. "The word for service is 'latreuo,' a priestly service" (Ryrie, <u>Revelation</u>, 123).

It will be something we are <u>equipped</u> to do and <u>enjoy</u> doing. Daniel was told that he would have his "allotted portion at the end of the age" (Dan. 12:13). Perhaps God has an administrative position reserved for Daniel. Our faithfulness in <u>this</u> <u>life</u> prepares us for higher service in <u>Heaven</u> (Wiersbe, 624). What kind of faithfulness are you exhibiting *now* for your future position? Are you being a good steward of all the natural and spiritual gifts and talents that God has given you? The real question is, "Are you serving Him *now*?"

2. We Will <u>See</u> Him.   22:4

"And they shall see His face, and His name shall be on their foreheads." We will see Him and proudly wear His identifying <u>mark</u> on our foreheads. Heaven would not be Heaven if we could not see <u>Jesus</u>. Seeing the One who loved me and died for me to rescue me from sin and Hell will be worth everything that I might have to suffer in this life. Most of those Christians to whom John was writing had *never seen Christ*. They had believed the word of the apostles. They longed to see the One who was raised from the dead and gave that same gift to them also. We will all see Him face to face.

"Face to face with Christ my Savior, face to face what will it be,
When with rapture I behold Him, Jesus Christ who died for me.

Only faintly now I see Him, with the darkling veil between,
But a blessed day is coming, when His glory shall be seen.

What rejoicing in His presence, when are banished grief and pain:
When the crooked ways are straightened, and the dark things shall be plain.

Face to face - oh, blissful moment! Face to face - to see and know;
Face to face with my Redeemer, Jesus Christ who loves me so.

Face to face I shall behold Him, far beyond the starry sky;
Face to face in all His glory, I shall see Him by and by!"
                    Carrie E. Breck, 1898

"And though you have not seen Him, you love Him, and though you do not see Him now, but believe in Him, you greatly rejoice with joy inexpressible and full of glory." (1 Pet. 1:8)

3. We Will Reign With Him.   22:5

"They shall reign." God's glory will illumine every corner of that place. Those who have served Him on earth will reign with Him in Heaven. We will be given positions of authority and honor to rule with Christ (cf. Matt. 19:28/ Rom. 5:17/ 1 Cor. 6:2-3/ Rev. 20:4,6).

4. We Will Live Forever With Him.   22:5

"And they shall reign *forever and ever*." One of the things that puts an end to fellowship down here is death. In Heaven we shall *never* die. We shall *never* grow old. We will live with Him and reign with Jesus Christ "forever and ever." Our reign and our fellowship will not be stopped because of death or any other factor. Our life there is not temporary, but eternal. We will have eternity to bask in the light of His glory and love.

Conclusion:

The New Heaven, the New Earth, and the New Jerusalem, will be the eternal domain of all those who have trusted Christ as Savior and have their names recorded in "the Lamb's book of life" (Rev. 21:27). It will be a place tailor made to satisfy and fulfill the greatest longings and desires of Christians for eternity. As the old spiritual says, "Everybody talkin' 'bout Heaven ain't goin' there." Only those who have *personally* and *publicly* placed their faith in Jesus and Him alone for the salvation of their souls will be granted entrance. In other words, you have to have a reservation. Make your reservation *today*! Invite some people along. It really will be worth it all!

LESSON 26
GOD'S LAST INVITATION
(REVELATION 22:6-21)

As we come to the final study in the book of Revelation, after having been warned about all the events and judgments of the Tribulation period, John extends an invitation to anyone who wishes to choose faith in Christ. After describing the beauties and the glories of the New Heaven, the New Earth, and the New Jerusalem, Jesus offers an open invitation to anyone who would like to go there and experience the joys and love and peace of that wonderful place He has prepared. In this last chapter of Revelation, chapter 22:6-21 we find this last invitation given in the Bible.

I. It is a <u>Positive</u> Invitation.   22:6

The question often comes about the <u>validity</u> of an invitation. Is it for real? What assurance do we have that God really means it? Notice the words that are used to affirm the validity of this invitation. "These words are <u>faithful</u> and <u>true</u>." "God ... sent His angel to show to His bond-servants the things which <u>must</u> shortly take place." There are no doubts. It is not tentative. It is presented as certain, sure, and trustworthy. God's Word is true and accurate (cf. 2 Tim. 3:16/ 2 Pet. 1:20-21/ John 17:17/ Ps. 19:7-9). You can <u>trust</u> God's Word, and you can accept God's invitation. God's Word is sure. God's promises are reliable. This invitation is positively real.

II. It is a <u>Pressing</u> Invitation.   22:6,7,10,12,20

A. Christ's Coming is Imminent.   22:6,10

His coming for the church is imminent, or impending. This means that it could happen at any moment. Verse 6 uses the word "shortly" to describe it. Verse 10 uses the word "near" to describe it. The emphasis here is that His coming could be soon, so a person had better make preparations for it right away. The hope of every generation of Christians from the first century until now is that Christ would come in their time. I'm glad that he delayed this long so that I might be saved as well. The signs of the times do indicate that His coming will be very soon.

Andrei Codrescu, speaking of Christians who believe in the imminent return of
Christ for His church, said on National Public Radio, "The evaporation of four

million (people) who believe in this crap would leave the world a better place" (Illustration Digest, Number 1, 1996, 16).

Of course, there have always been unbelievers who have scoffed at Jesus' promised return. Scoffers and mockers like to use these verses to say, "Where is the promise of His coming" (2 Pet. 3:4).

Peter answers that question very ably in 2 Peter 3:8-9, "But do not let this one fact escape your notice, beloved, that with the Lord one day is as a thousand years, and a thousand years as one day. The Lord is not slow about His promise, as some count slowness, but is patient toward you, not wishing for any to perish but for all to come to repentance." He is tarrying His coming so more people will have an opportunity to take advantage of His invitation.

Have you accepted His invitation yet? Daniel who lived before the Cross was told to seal up the words of his prophecy (Dan. 12:4), but John who lived after the Cross was told in verse 10 "Do not seal up the words of the prophecy of this book." Jesus wanted everyone to be aware of these coming events, and to respond to His open invitation.

B. Christ's Coming will be Sudden.   22:7,12,20

Three times in this chapter, Jesus affirms the facts of His historical and bodily return through the phrase, "I am coming quickly." This is a promise. It is not tentative. In John 14:3 He said "I will come again." He did not say, "I may come again." The word "quickly" refers to the manner of His coming. It means "suddenly." Several other passages underscore the suddenness of His coming.

1 Corinthians 15:52 says He will come, "In a moment, in the twinkling of an eye." Matthew 24:44 says "The Son of Man is coming at an hour when you do not think He will." Are you ready? When He comes it will be so sudden, that there won't be time for people to prepare. That is why the Bible says, "Now is 'the acceptable time,' behold now is 'the day of salvation'" (2 Cor. 6:2).

III. It is Priceless Invitation.   22:7,12,14

For those who are ready when death occurs or when Christ returns, it is priceless. It is an invitation to a fabulous reward.

A. Priceless because of the Promise of Happiness   22:7,14

There are two "blessed's" in these two verses. "Blessed" in the Scripture means "happy," or "receiver of happiness." Happy are those who are sufficiently ready when Christ comes. He describes *two* positive responses to God's invitation.

1. "He who *heeds* the words of the prophecy of this book."   22:7

"Heed" means to hear and respond in faith. Have you heeded the message of Revelation?

2. "Those who *wash* their robes."   22:14

This refers to genuine believers. Revelation 7:14 says, "These are the ones who come out of the great tribulation, and they have washed their robes and made them white in the blood of the Lamb." This symbolism refers to the fact that a person's record is wiped

<u>clean</u> forever the moment they *personally* put their faith in Jesus as their one and only Savior. This is how they prepared themselves for His coming.

Are You Washed in the Blood

"Have you been to Jesus for the cleansing power?
Are you washed in the blood of the Lamb?
Are you fully trusting in his grace this hour?
Are you washed in the blood of the Lamb?

Are you walking daily by the Savior's side?
Are you washed in the blood of the Lamb?
Do you rest each moment in the Crucified?
Are you washed in the blood of the Lamb?

When the Bridegroom cometh will your robes be white?
Are you washed in the blood of the Lamb?
Will your soul be ready for the mansion's bright,
And be washed in the blood of the Lamb?

Lay aside the garments that are stained with sin,
And be washed in the blood of the Lamb?
There's a fountain flowing for the soul unclean,
O, be washed in the blood of the Lamb?

Are you washed in the blood, in the soul cleansing blood of the Lamb?
Are your garments spotless? Are they white as snow?
Are you washed in the blood of the Lamb?
Elisha A. Hoffman, 1878

B. Priceless because of the Promise of <u>Reward</u> 22:12,14

1. "And my *reward* is with me to render to every man according to what he has done" (22:12).

God will reward people when He comes. There are degrees of <u>reward</u> and <u>punishment</u>. He will reward those who have served Him according to what they have done or not done. He will also punish wrongdoers according to what they have done.

This promise is a <u>comfort</u> to the saved and <u>terror</u> to the unsaved. Does Christ's coming comfort and encourage you, or does it frighten you?

2. "That they might have the right to the *tree of life*" (22:14).

This is the tree that was removed from the Garden of <u>Eden</u> after the sin of <u>Adam</u> and <u>Eve</u>. It was lost to mankind. It is recovered in Revelation 22:2 with its power to sustain

<u>life</u> and <u>health</u>. It will be available to all who have responded to God's invitation (cf. Rev. 2:7).

3. "They ... may enter by the gates into *the city*" (22:14).

Not everyone can enter that celestial city to enjoy its many benefits, only "those who wash their robes." This city is the New Jerusalem that is described so beautifully in 21:1-22:5.

IV. It is a <u>Pivotal</u> Invitation.   22:11,13-15, 18-19

It is a very serious invitation and is not to be taken lightly.

A. It is Pivotal because our destiny is fixed by our decision.   22:11

He will come so quickly that people will not have time to change their character. The "righteous" will go on being righteous throughout eternity. The "filthy" will be filthy throughout eternity. If a person refuses to respond to the message of Revelation, there is nothing more God can say to cause them to repent.

B. It is Pivotal because of the Person who offers it.   22:13

"I am the Alpha and the Omega." He is the most important person in the universe. He was here before anything was and will be here when everything is gone. Jesus is the Pivotal Person in all of history. Our entire calendar is established around His life. Everyone must make a decision concerning Him. Not to decide, is to decide against Him.

C. It is Pivotal because some are inside and some are outside.   22:14,15

Verse 14 describes those who "enter by the gates into the city." Verse 15 describes those who do not obtain entrance to the New Jerusalem. "Outside are the dogs (people of low character) and the sorcerers (those given to the occult and drugs) and the immoral persons and the murderers and the idolaters, and everyone who loves and practices lying." These sins are so commonplace today. People who know Christ should forsake the sins of their past by the power of the Holy Spirit. Consider that word "outside." How horrible it would be to be eternally outside of God's city and to be forever separated from God's grace, God's love, God's forgiveness, God's mercy, God's help, and God's family.

D. It is Pivotal because of the stern warning connected with it.   22:18-19

Revelation begins with a blessing on all who read it (1:3), and ends with a curse on all who deny the absolute truth of it (22:18-19).

Have people taken away from and diminished its meaning?

Yes! Let every *cult* and every self-proclaimed prophet who claims to receive a *new* revelation from God beware! Let every liberal preacher who minimizes this message beware!

Have people added some new revelation to it?

Yes! The Mormons have. The Jehovah Witnesses have. The Moonies have. Christian Science has. Dianetics has. Let every religious quack, cult, and racketeer beware! These words need to be taken seriously and literally. Our attitude needs to be one of humbly trying to do our best to interpret it correctly. We need to openly admit where our understanding ends and where our speculating begins (LaHaye, p. 321). Our confidence is that God sees the heart and can separate ignorance and immaturity from rebellion (Wiersbe, p. 625). But it is a horrible mistake to <u>add</u> to Revelation or any part of the Bible, to <u>deny</u> it, or to <u>ignore</u> it.

V. It is a <u>Personal</u> Invitation.   22:16-17

A. It is *from* a Person - <u>Jesus</u>.   22:16-17

"I, Jesus, have sent My angel to testify to you these things for the churches." He alone has the right to offer the invitation, because He alone has paid the price of <u>admission</u>. He is so earnest in offering this invitation, that here at the invitation He extends a <u>personal</u> appeal. It comes <u>directly</u> from *Jesus*, not from John, or from the angel. It is also extended by the *Holy Spirit* (v. 17). Perhaps He is speaking to your heart *today*. It is also extended by His Bride, the *Church* (v. 17). It is also extended by *individual believers*, ("let the *one* who hears say 'Come'" v.17). "We are ambassadors for Christ, as though God were entreating through us; we beg you on behalf of Christ, be reconciled to God" (2 Cor. 5:20).

B. It is *to* a Person - <u>You</u>.   22:17

1. "The one who is <u>thirsty</u>."

It is to the person who is "thirsty" for a <u>relationship</u> with God, to the person who is "thirsty" to have their sins <u>forgiven</u>, to the person who is longing for <u>meaning</u> and <u>purpose</u> in life. The great thirst of our soul, *cannot* be satisfied with alcohol, drugs, sex, parties, friends, work, hobbies, or anything else except a relationship with Christ. Only Jesus can satisfy your thirst.

2. "The one who <u>wishes</u>."

The King James version says, "whosoever will." That is the required response to His invitation. It is an act of your <u>will</u> to put your trust in Jesus. He cannot save you against your will.

You must personally choose to ask Jesus to save you. You supply the thirst, and He supplies the "water of life." He says this water is "without cost." It is <u>free</u> to the recipient. It cost <u>Jesus</u> the ultimate sacrifice. Peter described it this way.

"You were ... redeemed ... with the precious blood, as of a lamb unblemished and spotless, the blood of Christ" (1 Pet. 1:19).

Conclusion:

The closing words of this book in 22:20-21 contain the Lord's promise and the believer's response.

1. A Closing Promise from *Jesus*.

"Yes, I am coming quickly" (v.20). Here Jesus repeats the promise given in verses 7 and 12. It is said three times for emphasis. It is His assurance that it *will* come to pass. These are the last recorded words of Jesus. It is an encouragement to every believer, and a warning to every unbeliever.

2. A Closing Affirmation from *John*.

"Amen. Come, Lord Jesus" (v.20). John echoes the response of every Christian to the message of Christ's return. "Amen" means "so be it." It stands for whole hearted agreement with the message that has been heard.

We have no need to fear at His coming. Everyone of us ought to be able to join with a hearty and enthusiastic "Amen" at the thought of Jesus coming back for His own.

3. A Closing Blessing for all *Christians*.

"The grace of the Lord Jesus be with all" (v.21). John's desire and prayer for every Christian and reader of this book is that God's enabling and sustaining grace would attend every believer until Christ's return. May His amazing grace enable *you* to serve Him fully and faithfully, and sustain you in every trial and circumstance of life...

Till He Comes!

APPENDIX #1   GOD'S TIMELINE FOR HUMANITY

Dr. Kelly Carr
Appendix 1

God's Timeline for Humanity

(Human History is not a circle of futility. It is linear. It has a destination. God has a plan for His creation.)

(You Are Here)

(Human Rebellion and God's Grace are both Evident in Every Period.)

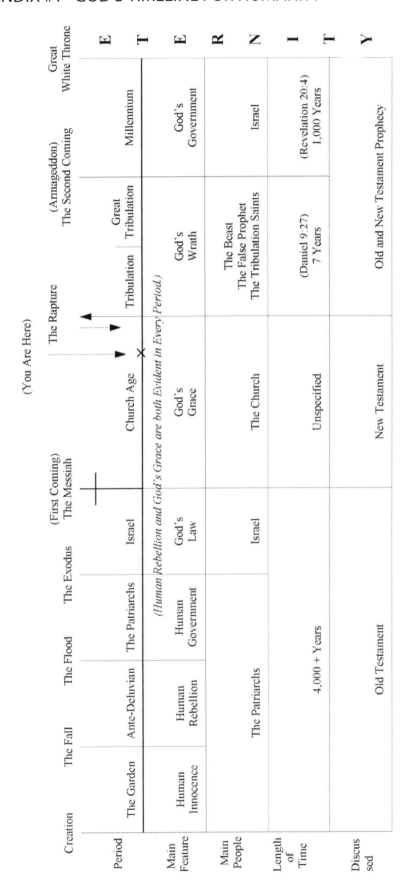

Period	Creation / The Garden	The Fall / Ante-Deluvian	The Flood / The Patriarchs	The Exodus	Israel (First Coming) The Messiah	Church Age The Rapture	Tribulation (Armageddon) The Second Coming	Great White Throne
							Great Tribulation	Millennium
Main Feature	Human Innocence	Human Rebellion	Human Government		God's Law	God's Grace	God's Wrath	God's Government
Main People		The Patriarchs			Israel	The Church	The Beast / The False Prophet / The Tribulation Saints	Israel
Length of Time		4,000 + Years				Unspecified	(Daniel 9:27) 7 Years	(Revelation 20:4) 1,000 Years
Discussed		Old Testament				New Testament		Old and New Testament Prophecy

ETERNITY

APPENDIX #2 REVELATION: BOOK OF MYSTERY AND MAJESTY

Revelation: Book of Mystery and Majesty

WRITER: Apostle John (1:1,4,9)
DATE: A.D. 95 from Patmos (1:9)
KEY VERSE: 1:19
KEY WORDS: throne (44x), lamb (29x),
similar (21x), thousand (19x), dragon (13x)

Prelude to the End	1:1-8	Prologue	
A Vision of Christ	1:9-20	"The things which you have seen"	A Look at some Present Realities — Chapters 1-3
Letters to the Seven Churches	2-3	"The things which are"	
The Throne Room of Heaven	4	A Look into the Heavenlies — Chapters 4-5	
The Worship of Heaven	5		
Seal Judgments	6	7 Seals — Chapter 6	A Look at the Personalities and Events of the Tribulation — Chapters 6-19
144,000 Sealed	7		
Trumpet Judgments	8-9	7 Trumpets — Chapters 8-9	
The Bitter Book	10		
The Two Witnesses	11		
Public Enemy #1 (The Dragon)	12		
The Mark of the Beast	13		
Six Postcards from the Future	14		
The Song of Victory	15	7 Bowls — Chapters 15-16	
Bowl Judgments	16		
Destruction of the Harlot	17		
Destruction of Babylon	18		
The Second Coming of Christ	19		
The Millenium	20	A Look at some Final Things — Chapters 20-22	
The New Jerusalem	21-22:5		
God's Last Invitation	22:6-21	Epilogue	

Rapture ⇨

Second Coming ⇨

"The things which shall take place after these things"

APPENDIX #3   THE SEVEN "BEATITUDES" OF REVELATION

Dr. Kelly Carr
Appendix 3

The Seven "Beatitudes" of Revelation

There are seven separate beatitudes, or blessings, in the book of Revelation. Each one contains a blessing for some particular activity and gives the reason for it. Each blessing is dependent upon the individual's response of faith in and obedience to the message of Revelation.

1st Beatitude	2nd Beatitude	3rd Beatitude	4th Beatitude	5th Beatitude	6th Beatitude	7th Beatitude
Revelation 1:3	Revelation 14:13	Revelation 16:15	Revelation 19:9	Revelation 20:6	Revelation 22:7	Revelation 22:14
Blessed is he who reads and those who hear the words of the prophecy, and heed the things which are written in it; for the time is near.	*And I heard a voice from heaven, saying, "Write, 'Blessed are the dead who die in the Lord from now on!'" "Yes," says the Spirit, "that they may rest from their labors, for their deeds follow with them."*	*("Behold, I am coming like a thief. Blessed is the one who stays awake and keeps his garments, lest he walk about naked and men see his shame.")*	*And he said to me, "Write, 'Blessed are those who are invited to the marriage supper of the Lamb.'" And he said to me, "These are the true words of God."*	*Blessed and holy is the one who has a part in the first resurrection; over these the second death has no power, but they will be priests of God and of Christ and will reign with Him for a thousand years.*	*"And behold, I am coming quickly. Blessed is he who heeds the words of the prophecy of this book."*	*Blessed are those who wash their robes, that they may have the right to the tree of life, and may enter by the gates into the city.*
The Blessed Activity	The Blessed Activity	The Blessed Activity	The Blessed Activity	The Blessed Activity	The Blessed Activity	The Blessed Activity
Reading and Rightly Responding to the message of Revelation	Dying in a Right Relationship with Jesus Christ	Living in Constant Readiness for Christ's Return	Being a Participant at the Marriage Supper of the Lamb	Being a Participant in the First Resurrection	Responding Rightly to the message of Revelation	Being saved and thus righteous and fit for Heaven
The Reason	The Reason	The Reason	The Reason	The Reason	The Reason	The Reason
Because the Prophecy may be fulfilled at any moment.	Because they will receive rest and rewards	Because they will not be ashamed to meet Christ when He comes	Because this prophecy will be fulfilled	Because they will have authority in Christ's Kingdom and will escape eternal judgment	Because Christ is really coming in a very sudden manner	Because they will have access to eternal life in the New Jerusalem

APPENDIX #4   THE SEVEN CHURCHES OF REVELATION

The Seven Churches of Revelation

	Ephesus 2:1-7	Smyrna 2:8-11	Pergamum 2:12-17	Thyatira 2:18-29	Sardis 3:1-6	Philadelphia 3:7-13	Laodicea 3:14-22
Location							
Chief Characteristic	The *Loveless* Church	The *Longsuffering* Church	The *Lax* Church	The *Licentious* Church	The *Lazy* Church	The *Loyal* Church	The *Lukewarm* Church
The Lord's Character Before His Church	He holds the seven stars in His right hand and He walks among the seven golden lampstands.	He is the eternal Christ, "the first and the last," and the resurrected Christ, "who was dead and has come to life."	He is Christ the judge "who has the sharp two-edged sword."	He is the "Son of God" (deity), has "eyes like a flame of fire" (discerning), and "feet like burnished bronze" (crushing).	He has the fullness of the Spirit, "the seven spirits," and He is sovereign, possessing the "seven stars."	He alone is "holy." He is "true" or genuine, and He has the keys, symbolizing His authority.	He is the "Amen" (reliable). He is God's authentic "witness," and He is the "beginning of the creation of God."
The Lord's Commendation for His Church	good works, hard work, endurance, intolerance of false teachers, discernment, stamina, opposition to cults	They remained faithful in spite of persecutions such as "tribulation," "poverty," and "blasphemy."	They held fast to Jesus' name and did not deny their faith in Him in spite of living near "Satan's throne."	They were active ("deeds"), loving, strong in faith, serving, persevering, and progressive.	No Commendation	They had some power in their ministry, they had "kept" His word, and had not "denied" His name.	No Commendation
The Lord's Complaint against His Church	"You have left your first love."	No Complaints	Some in the church held to the teaching of Balaam and the Nicolaitans resulting in idolatry and immorality.	They tolerated false doctrine, and a false teacher called "Jezebel." She led people into idolatry and immorality.	They were asleep and should "wake up," weak and should be strengthened. Their work was unfinished.	No Complaints	They were "lukewarm," and they were proud in thinking they had "need of nothing."
The Lord's Command for His Church	Remember... Repent... Return...	"Do not fear" "Be faithful until death"	Those who were compromising with pagan idolatry and immorality should "repent" or expect swift judgment.	Her followers should "repent" to avoid judgment. The rest should "hold fast" to what they have.	"Wake up" "Strengthen" "Remember" "Keep" "Repent"	"Hold fast what you have." They should keep on doing their best, and go through the door He would open.	"Be Zealous" (literally, "be boiling") "Repent"
The Lord's Challenge for His Church	The overcomer will eat of the "tree of life"	The overcomer will receive the crown of life, and escape the second death.	The overcomer will receive "hidden manna," "a white stone," and "a new name," sustenance and forgiveness.	The overcomer will receive "authority over the nations," and fellowship with "the morning star."	The overcomer will wear "white garments," have his name in the "book of life" and confessed before God.	The overcomer will become a "pillar in the temple of My God," and be personally marked by God's name.	The overcomer will "sit down with Me on My throne."

APPENDIX #5   PREMILLENNIAL VIEWS OF THE RAPTURE

Dr. Kelly Carr
Appendix 5

Premillennial Views of the Rapture

Rapture: (Greek = harpazo) literally "to catch away," "to snatch," "to seize," cf. 1 Thess. 4:17 translated "caught up"
Other uses of the word: Acts 8:30/ 2 Cor. 12:2, 4
Key Scriptures: 1 Thess. 4:13-17/ 1 Cor. 15:51, 52

Definition: The sudden removal of all believers from the earth by the Lord. Dead believers will be resurrected and living believers will be taken up alive. All will be immediately translated into new immortal bodies.

	Pretribulation Rapture	Midtribulation Rapture	Posttribulation Rapture	Partial Rapture
Time of the Rapture	The Rapture will occur *before* the 7 year tribulation begins.	The Rapture will occur at the *mid-point* of the 7 year tribulation.	The Rapture will occur *near the end* of the 7 year tribulation.	Not concerned about the time of the Rapture.
Participants of the Rapture	All believers	All believers	All believers	Only "watchful" believers
Scriptural Support	John 14:2-3/ Acts 1:11/ 1 Cor. 1:7/ 15:51-52/ Phil. 3:20-21/ 1 Thess. 1:9-10/ 4:16-17/ Tit. 2:13/ Jam. 5:8-9/ Rev. 3:10/ 22:17-22	Dan. 9:27/ Matt. 24:21/ Rev. 11	Matt. 24:9-11/ Mark 13:9-13/ Luke 23:27-31/ John 15:18-19/ 16:1-2,33	Matt. 24:41-42/ Luke 21:36/ Phil. 3:20/ 2 Tim. 4:8/ Tit. 2:13/ Heb. 9:28
Essentials of the Position	1. Distinguishes between the Rapture and the Second Coming. 2. Clear distinction between the Church and Israel. 3. Rapture is imminent	1. Distinguishes between the Rapture and the Second Coming. 2. Unclear distinction between the Church and Israel. 3. Rapture is not imminent.	1. The Rapture and the Second Coming are the same event. 2. No distinction between the Church and Israel. 3. Rapture is not imminent.	1. Implies that salvation is incomplete. 2. Denies the unity of the Body of Christ. 3. Implies a partial resurrection.

APPENDIX #6   THREE MAJOR VIEWS OF THE MILLENNIUM

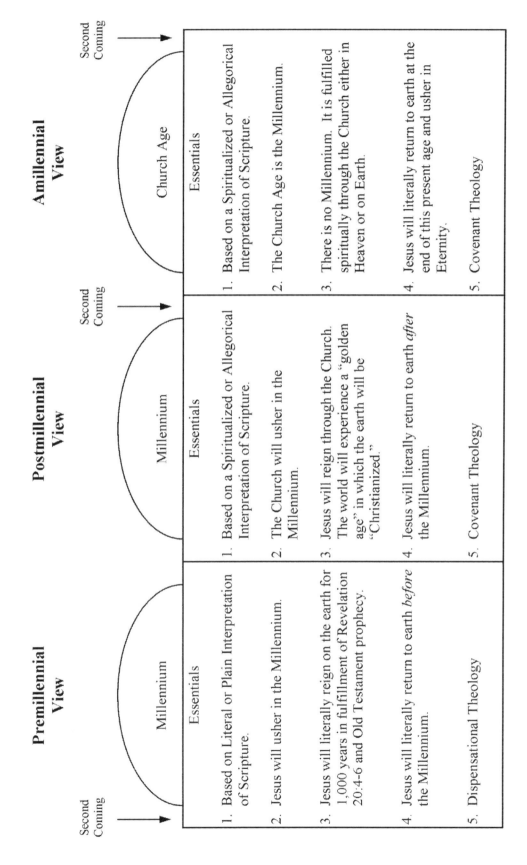

SOURCES TO CONSULT

Barclay, William. The Revelation of John: Volume 1. Philadelphia: The Westminster Press, 1976.

Dyer, Charles H. The Rise of Babylon: Sign of the End Times. Wheaton: Tyndale House Publishers, 1991.

Havner, Vance. Messages on Revelation. Grand Rapids: Baker Book House, 1958.

Ironside, H. A. Revelation. Neptune, New Jersey: Loizeaux Brothers, 1920.

Johnson, Alan F. "Revelation," in The Expositor's Bible Commentary, Volume 12. Frank E. Gaebelein, ed. Grand Rapids: Zondervan Publishing House, 1981.

LaHaye, Tim. Revelation: Illustrated and Made Plain. Grand Rapids: Zondervan Publishing House, 1973.

Lalonde, Peter. One World Under Anti-Christ. Eugene, Oregon: Harvest House Publishers, 1991.

Lalonde, Peter, and Paul Lalonde. Racing Toward the Mark of the Beast. Eugene, Oregon: Harvest House Publishers, 1994.

McGee, J. Vernon. Reveling Through Revelation: Part 1 and 2. Los Angeles: Church of the Open Door, 1962.

Pentecost, J. Dwight. Things to Come. Grand Rapids: Zondervan Publishing House, 1958.

Phillips, John. Exploring Revelation. Chicago: Moody Press, 1974.

Ryrie, Charles C. Basic Theology. Wheaton, Illinois: Victor Books, 1986.

Ryrie, Charles C. Revelation. Chicago: Moody Press, 1968.

Ryrie, Charles C. What You Should Know About The Rapture. Chicago: Moody Press, 1981.

Smith, J. B. A Revelation of Jesus Christ. Scottsdale, Pennsylvania: Mennonite Publishing House, 1961.

Strauss, Lehman. The Book of Revelation. Neptune, New Jersey: Loizeaux Brothers, 1964.

Swindoll, Charles R. Letters to the Churches ... Then and Now. Fullerton, California: Insight For Living, 1981.

Walvoord, John F. "Revelation," in <u>The Bible Knowledge Commentary</u>. Edited by John F. Walvoord and Roy B. Zuck. Wheaton: Victor Books, 1983.

Walvoord, John F. <u>The Revelation of Jesus Christ</u>. Chicago: Moody Press, 1966.

Wiersbe, Warren W. "Revelation," in <u>The Bible Exposition Commentary</u>: <u>Volume 2</u>. Wheaton: Victor Books, 1989.

Willmington, H. L. <u>The King is Coming</u>. Wheaton: Tyndale House Publishers, 1973.

Periodicals and Notes

Bailey, Mark. Class Notes. Dallas Theological Seminary.

Sevener, Harold A. "The Temple" in <u>The Chosen People</u>. Nov. 1992, Dec. 1992.

SUGGESTED READING

(From the Kindle Version)

Revelation: Book of Mystery and Majesty by Dr. Kelly Carr, This is a <u>**Revelation Bible study guide**</u> on the New Testament book of Revelation. This study guide is great for personal study or group study. There is also an accompanying "fill in the blank" guide for students. It is conveniently divided into 26 lessons for easy study. Click below to go and see it now at the Amazon Kindle bookstore.

<u>**Revelation Book of Mystery and Majesty by Dr. Kelly Carr Foreword by Dr. Jerry Falwell**</u>

A Guidebook for Searchers Is There Really Evidence Behind Our Faith? Is a great little book that answers six questions that seekers or searchers are looking for today. Questions like "Is There Really a God?," "Can We Really Trust an Ancient Book?," "Is There Really Life After Death?," and more. It is brief and packed with tons of information. It is also handy if you have a friend who is struggling with <u>agnosticism</u>, or if you are looking for <u>evidence for God</u>.

Click below to go and see it now at the Amazon Kindle bookstore.

<u>**A Guidebook for Searchers Is There Evidence Behind Our Faith? By Kelly Carr, Foreword by Dr. Mark Bailey**</u>

<u>**Daily Prayer Journal: A Personal Guide to Daily Devotions**</u> by Dr. Kelly Carr, This prayer and reading guide is designed to help people who are looking for an organized way to have a daily time with God. It has a section with a daily checklist and a list of specific topics to pray for each day of the week. It also come with several sections such as how to study the Bible, how to pray, how to read the Bible in a year, how to witness to a friend, and more Why not give this <u>prayer book</u> as a gift.

<u>**Basic Theology: A Popular Systematic Guide to Understanding Biblical Truth [Hardcover]**</u>
<u>**Basic Theology: A Popular Systematic Guide to Understanding Biblical Truth [Kindle]**</u>

Charles C. Ryrie has a created a library of theology in one easy location. Perhaps no one else in America has the unique ability to take complex subjects and explain them in simple and easy to understand language. He also brings the most relevant scripture passages to bear on each theological topic. I would encourage you to get the hard copy and keep it close by. However, a friend of mine recently purchased the Kindle version and loves it.

<u>**The Purpose-Driven Life [Hardcover]**</u>
<u>**The Purpose-Driven Life [Kindle]**</u>

Rick Warren's new classic, **The Purpose Driven Life**, is not only full of truth presented in a simple way, but is incredibly inspirational. He has a way of saying things that makes them understandable and memorable. I encourage anyone to read through any of his well written books. BTW Try his new study called **"40 Days In The Word."**

Face to Face: Praying the Scriptures for Intimate Worship [Paperback]
Or
Face to Face: Praying the Scriptures for Spiritual Growth: [Kindle Edition]
I have benefitted from Kenneth Boa's books on prayer as many Christians have and I think you will, as well.

Partners in Prayer [Paperback]
John Maxwell's great little book, **Partners in Prayer** is an excellent guide to help Christians know how to pray for their Pastor. Even more, it is an important tool that Pastors can use to recruit and inspire an army of prayer warriors.

Remember, if you do not have a Kindle, yet you can still download the Kindle reader for free on your computer, tablet, iPod, iPad, iPhone or smart phone and be able to download, read, and have handy copies of all your Amazon books.

BTW, I really love my **Kindle Fire. (Click Here to See How Many Books Your Kindle Fire Library will Hold.)**

Thanks again,

Kelly Carr

www.HigherPurposeMinistries.com

PS If you have a friend whose child is beginning to stutter, this Kindle eBook has great insights to help prevent stuttering in children.

Stutter Prevention Secrets: How Parents and Teachers Can Help Prevent Stuttering (or Stammering) In Children by Leon Lassers

ABOUT THE AUTHOR

Kelly Carr grew up on the dusty plains of West Texas surrounded by family and a group of good and hardy people. He came from a family of educators on both sides of the family tree, but took a slightly different path which led him into ministry. Kelly is committed to lifelong learning and enjoys writing on a variety of topics.

Dr. Carr holds degrees in ministry from Liberty University, Dallas Theological Seminary, and Southwestern Baptist Theological Seminary. He has been involved in church ministry as a Pastor, Church Planter, Executive Pastor, Minister of Education and Youth Pastor for more than 25 years, also holding leadership positions at the community, area, state and national level of his denomination. He currently ministers in Greenville, Texas and lives with his beautiful wife of 29 years and his three awesome children.

Made in the USA
San Bernardino, CA
21 October 2015